Better Homes and Gardens®

TRELLISES ARBORS & PERGOLAS

IDEAS AND PLANS FOR GARDEN STRUCTURES

Meredith® Books

Des Moines, Iowa

Better Homes and Gardens® Trellises, Arbors & Pergolas
Editor: Larry Johnston
Contributing Writers: Joe Hawkins, Jim Hufnagel
Senior Associate Design Director: John Eric Seid
Contributing Designer: Tim Abramowitz
Assistant Editor: Harijs Priekulis
Copy Chief: Terri Fredrickson
Copy and Production Editor: Victoria Forlini
Editorial Operations Manager: Karen Schirm
Managers, Book Production: Pam Kvitne,
    Marjorie J. Schenkelberg, Rick von Holdt
Contributing Copy Editor: Steve Hallam
Technical Proofreader: Griffin Wall
Contributing Proofreaders: Heidi Johnson, Terri Krueger,
    Courtenay Wolf,
Indexer: Barbara L. Klein
Editorial and Design Assistants: Renee E. McAtee,
    Karen McFadden

**Additional Editorial Contributions from
    Art Rep Services**
Director: Chip Nadeau
Designer: lk Design
Illustrator: Dave Brandon
Photographer: InsideOut Studio

Meredith® Books
Editor in Chief: Linda Raglan Cunningham
Design Director: Matt Strelecki
Executive Editor, Gardening and Home Improvement:
    Benjamin W. Allen
Executive Editor, Home Improvement: Larry Erickson

Publisher: James D. Blume
Executive Director, Marketing: Jeffrey Myers
Executive Director, New Business Development:
    Todd M. Davis
Executive Director, Sales: Ken Zagor
Director, Operations: George A. Susral
Director, Production: Douglas M. Johnston
Business Director: Jim Leonard

Vice President and General Manager: Douglas J. Guendel

Meredith Publishing Group
President, Publishing Group: Stephen M. Lacy
Vice President-Publishing Director: Bob Mate

Meredith Corporation
Chairman and Chief Executive Officer: William T. Kerr

In Memoriam: E. T. Meredith III (1933-2003)

Photographers
    (Photographers credited may retain copyright ©
    to the listed photographs.)
    L = Left, R = Right, C = Center, B = Bottom,
    T = Top
Hetherington Photography: 49TR
InsideOut Studio: 128, 129, 130, 131, 134, 135, 138

TABLE OF CONTENTS

CHAPTER HIGHLIGHTS

Trellises, arbors, and pergolas are perfect choices for adding vertical structure and climbing plants to your yard. In this chapter you will find some great structures, examples of plants you might want to use, and lots of outdoor decorating ideas. Personalize your yard with the ones that best fit your needs and personality.

FIND YOUR INSPIRATION

Aspire to new heights

Trellises, arbors, and pergolas will transform your yard into a relaxing retreat with a garden that reaches for the sky.

You can completely cover your structures with climbing plants and bountiful blooms or leave them bare to reveal their architectural designs. Either way, trellises, arbors, and pergolas offer shade and shelter and add points of interest to any garden.

Let the ideas in this chapter inspire you to follow your own sense of style and to be as passionate about beautifying your landscape as you are about decorating your home. Whether your taste leans toward traditional, cottage, rustic, or contemporary style, you can integrate that style into your structure. As you look at the structures, consider which climbing plants you might like to grow. (Chapter 3 takes a detailed look at plants.)

There's plenty of information in this chapter to help you get started with planning and design.

Start with a look at structures on the next page.

ARBORS

Add romance to a garden with an arbor.

Whether old-fashioned or modern in style, these focal-point structures are built to be experienced up close, so they draw people to them and make you and your guests want to linger longer in the garden.

What, exactly, is an arbor? Some people incorrectly refer to arbors as pergolas. (You'll see some fine examples of pergolas starting on page 16 of this chapter.) While some designs may blur the distinction between these types of structures, an arbor is simply an arch that plants can grow on. A pergola is larger and usually has several columns that support an overhead structure where plants and vines can grow.

▲ The simple white arbor stands in contrast to a riotous display of colorful flowers.

You'll find arbor kits available at any number of home and garden centers, from catalogs, or online. However, a homeowner with average carpentry skills and basic tools can easily build a custom structure like those shown in chapter 2 of this book.

If you are the do-it-yourself type, you can draw up a master plan for the design of your home's landscape. Many books, videos, and websites offer excellent advice on landscape design, and you may enjoy creating a design of your own. Or have a professional develop a plan for your yard, based on your ideas. Either way, it's smart to have an overall plan before you commit to a spot for building an arbor or other structure in your yard. a

▼ A blooming vine engulfs and softens the entryway.

◀ A repeating theme of three matching arbors adds interest to this garden.

▼ Even a simple structure like this entry arbor can provide a warm welcome as it individualizes your home.

Before you build, ask yourself a few questions

Here are things to consider before building:

■ What do you hope to accomplish with this structure? You may simply want to use it as a focal point or to mark a transition between spaces, such as the sidewalk and the yard, or two different areas within the garden. It could also be a destination that includes a seating area or swing.

■ What architectural style would look best and match your personality? Traditional, cottage, rustic, and contemporary are some of the styles you might consider. Find more about determining your style on pages 28–35.

■ What types of finish and wood or other materials should you use? Lumber (pressure-

treated or naturally rot-resistant species such as redwood or cedar), branches and twigs, metal, and even some types of plastics all have their advantages and disadvantages and can help set the mood of your structure. Many arbors are painted white, but they can also be stained or left to weather naturally. You'll find more on materials and finishes in "Starting Point" on pages 44–49 and in chapter 4, beginning on page 128.

ROOM DIVIDERS

Whether acting as a passage to another area in your garden or defining the real entry to your home, most arbors look best standing alone in a yard. However, don't miss the opportunity to make an entry a focal point by building an arbor through a fence, hedge, or wall.

Depending on its purpose, you may want to include a gate in your attached arbor, right, or make it a restful spot to relax by including a seating area, below. Most arbors look great engulfed in blooms, while others stand on their own architectural merit.

Arbors can help transform an area of your yard into an outdoor room. You can develop a plan for your yard based on separate rooms. Like your home's floor plan, the outdoor spaces should follow a logical progression from room to room,

One garden room might be a shady and private retreat. Another can be like

■ The arbors, *above* and *below left,* are built as part of the fences around them. Those on the *opposite page* stand alone in the landscape. Either freestanding or attached arbors look good with or without plants growing on them.

a family room—a spacious, open area where you can host a large party. Structures like those shown here can act as dividers between these rooms, lending a sense of drama and intrigue to what lies beyond.

When planning for garden rooms, consider the activities they will accommodate, such as the ones listed on the next page.

■ **Child's play.** You might want to locate a children's play area where it can easily be supervised from the deck or patio.

■ **Dining and entertaining.** Colorful flowers nearby and some shade overhead make a dining area more pleasant for you and guests. You'll use the outdoor dining area more often with the convenience of easy serving access from the kitchen. In warmer climates, you might want to include an outdoor kitchen in your plans.

■ **Relaxation.** While away a lazy summer afternoon napping on comfortable outdoor furniture or a hammock. Build a seating area around a fire pit or fountain. A pool or spa area is another possibility.

■ **Gardening and yard work.** A more utilitarian space can be created for potting plants and storing garden tools. Or create a hidden garden that includes a wide assortment of your favorite plantings.

■ **Endless possibilities.** Only your imagination and budget limit the outdoor rooms you can create around your home to suit your lifestyle.

▲ A simple arched arbor provides a portal through the hedge to another part of the yard. The gate adds just enough privacy and security.

▶ A rose-covered arbor gives guests a warm welcome at the front sidewalk. Without a gate, the arbor draws visitors right in.

PRIVATE GETAWAYS

▲ A winding pathway to this arbor beckons guests to investigate what is clearly another garden room.

If your dream is to create one or more rooms in your yard where you can get away from it all, an arbor can play an important role. Whether acting as a gateway to the getaway or as the final destination, arbors like those shown here are up to the task.

As you plan a getaway in your yard, think about how you would spend time there, and ask yourself these questions: Do you want something totally secluded, where you can shut out the worries of the world while reading a good book? Are you looking for a formal space where you can sip tea peacefully? Are you looking for a shady space where you can serve a midday meal? Do you want an open area where kids and pets can romp all day?

Think of the space as a destination. Whether the getaway feels like a separate room or is simply a place to put a couple of chairs and an umbrella, it should evoke the feeling that it's actually a place where you want to go.

Make a list of your priorities; then start to make choices. You'll soon have planned a

▶ This large arbor is a focal point for the yard and marks the transition from one area to another.

◀ Roses ramble over this rustic arbor, creating an enchanting entry to a restful get-away spot.

retreat that fits your needs and is yours in every way. Does your yard include a certain area that naturally sets it apart from other parts of the landscape? Perhaps there's a sunken area, sunny spot, or heavily shaded area that lends itself to becoming an inviting getaway. Do you have only open expanses of lawn? Create the illusion of a secret garden by growing hedges and including garden structures or screens with vines growing over them. The vines will eventually create a lush roof overhead.

After you've found such a space–or have created it from scratch–you can accessorize it with outdoor furniture that will reinforce the mood you hope to establish. Lay out pathways of stone, brick, or turf to guide guests to the retreat and set the tone for the experience.

For instance, a neatly laid out brick pathway might signal that you are about to enter a formal tea garden framed with boxwood hedges and traditional-style structures. Or add mystery with a winding path of stones surrounded by ornamental grasses that veil the retreat until you reach it.

▼ Sometimes the arbor itself becomes the getaway. This one is surrounded by blooms and features a comfy bench.

TRELLISES

Trellises are timeless.

Structures designed and built solely to support plants date back to the mists of history. (Even ancient Egyptian hieroglyphics have images of grapes growing on them.) Today, trellises are as useful as ever and are the easiest way to bring height to your garden.

Trellises allow you to grow climbing plants that will add beauty and interest to your yard or they can screen off unsightly areas. They can be as simple as a plain piece of lattice attached to the side of your house or as complex as an intricate garden centerpiece structure. They can go almost anywhere in the landscape. If you live in an area where winters are cold, trellises also add architectural interest to your views long after the plants have died back.

Some trellises are freestanding; others may be attached to arbors or other structures. A plain fence or a wall (including a garden wall or an exterior wall of your house or other building) is a natural place to locate a trellis. Think of such

▲ Even without vines, the simple, yet stylish, trellis looks great attached to the column of a pergola. Eventually, vines will climb the column.

spaces as blank canvases for you to dress up with foliage and color. Roses and many vines and other climbing plants are available to grow on your trellis. For more information about selecting plants for trellises in your yard, see "Growth Opportunities" on pages 20–27.

For fast coverage in the first season of your trellis, plant a quick-growing annual vine (see page 23) that will start the show while slower-growing

■ Attached to an exterior wall of a home, *above*, or to the posts of a pergola, *right*, trellises can add vertical interest to the landscape.

perennial climbers are getting established. Chapter 3 of this book offers more information on climbing plants and roses.

The design of a trellis is limited only by your imagination, from white wood trellises in a formal or cottage-style garden to a bamboo or plastic structure in a more unconventional setting. An important consideration in the design you select is the types of plants that will be growing on the trellis.

◄ A simple design of bamboo poles lashed together can make an interesting and effective trellis.

LEARNING TO LOVE LATTICE

▲ Vines climb on this three-section lattice screen, creating a private and secluded spot to sit in the yard.

Twining vines like morning glories will wind along any straight support, while tendriled climbers such as clematis produce tiny stems that latch onto supports. They clamber best up mesh or on strings. Thorns don't help roses latch onto trellises, and these plants are best lashed to a trellis with loose ties as they grow. Another type of trellis can be used to train fruit or vegetable plants to grow in a pleasing pattern while still providing produce. This type of gardening, known as espalier, is discussed on pages 26–27.

Trellises also can cover up unsightly features in your landscape, such as utility meters, air-conditioning units, power transformers, and trash cans. Although you have to have them, by strategically placing trellises you can soften the impact of these utilitarian eyesores. Check with the utility company to find out about regulations governing such cover-ups, especially for utility meters, which must be accessible for readings.

▶ A bamboo trellis dresses up a plain fence and adds an exotic touch to this landscape.

◀ The lattice
screen helps
make this section
of the garden a
separate room.

For long-lasting wood trellises, use rot-resistant materials such as pressure-treated lumber, cedar, or redwood. Apply exterior-grade stain or primer and paint before you assemble the pieces to avoid difficult brushwork later. Trellises may also be constructed of plastic, wire, copper pipe, twigs, or other materials.

Set your trellis securely into the ground or attach it to some permanent structure, such as a house wall or fence. Combined with a strong gust of wind, the weight of many mature vines could cause your trellis to come crashing down if it is not properly secured. For slender trellises that are stuck into the ground, drive steel rods into the soil near the base of the trellis and lash the trellis to the rods with wire.

Plans for trellises you can build are shown in chapter 2. If you don't want to build a trellis, you can often find a good selection of prebuilt trellises for sale in home or garden centers, in catalogs, at flea markets, or on the Internet.

▶ A black grid trellis injects a striking design element into what would otherwise be a blank white wall on a stylish patio.

PERGOLAS

▲ Gently arched beams topped with 2×2s form a shade-giving roof over a freestanding 8×8-foot deck. Lattice panels enclose the lower sides.

Sometimes, especially when the hot summer sun beats down, it's nice to have it made in the shade. And that's a primary benefit of adding a pergola to your landscape—you can create your own shady retreat.

Pergolas can also be beautiful features in their own right, connecting one garden area to another, dividing the landscape into separate outdoor rooms, framing a view, or leading guests' gazes across your yard. Their other function is to provide support and an attractive spot for roses and other types of climbing plants—even fruit and vegetables—to grow.

Usually more substantial than an arbor but not as confining as a gazebo, a pergola may be as simple as an overhead structure attached to the back of your house to cover a deck. Or it might be a grand, freestanding structure that is the main focal point of a yard. Pergolas are especially effective over paved areas, such as paths, courtyards, and patios.

If you are shading a sitting or dining area, consider wind and sun patterns, especially during summer months, and try to take these variables into account in the structure's design. Trellises or materials like lattice can be included on one or more sides of a pergola, adding to the tunnel effect and blocking unwanted views. If you are starting from scratch on your garden design at a new home, a pergola can be the element that sets the stage for the rest of your landscape design drama. If your landscape is already well developed, a pergola could be the element that ties it all together.

■ Small in scale, but still a pergola, the structure *above left* adds class to a corner of the deck. Classic columns support the pergola *above right* and create a dining space in front of the pool house.

◄ More inviting than a welcome mat, this simple pergola beckons guests to enjoy the home's gardens as it guides visitors to the front door.

COMFORT FROM HIGH STYLE

▼ The tall pergola in this narrow side yard is in perfect scale with the home and adds an impressive and shady resting spot along the path.

Pergolas typically have a framework of beams and rafters overhead that is supported by posts or columns. Even without plants, a pergola can provide comfortable shade where there's not enough natural shade. The amount of sunlight that filters through depends on the size and placement of the boards on top. Just as with arbors and trellises, building a pergola is a project that many do-it-yourselfers may be able to tackle.

You're less likely to find kits for pergolas like the ones that are sold for arbors or trellises. But many design and construction firms can help you with this type of project. If you decide to tackle the project yourself, check with your local building department to see if you need a building permit. If you hire out the work, make sure the builder takes care of permits for you.

Plans for pergolas are shown in chapter 2. You can design your own with ideas from magazines or hire a designer. It's usually best to

▲ Light and airy in design, this pergola imparts a sense of being inside an enclosed pavilion.

◄ Not quite a pergola (there's no roof) but more than an arbor (it spans the entire deck), this structure nicely frames the garden view.

▼ The rafters shade a swing hanging from the upper beams of this pergola. Eventually, vines covering the structure will provide even more shade.

keep the design simple, and if you are using more than one pergola (or other structures) in a landscape, stick to one style that complements your house and is in proportion to its size. Also decide whether you want a private retreat or a grand gathering space. and whether it should be formal or informal.

Most pergolas are made of wood, but metal, vinyl, and other alternatives are also available. For longevity, use woods that are naturally rot-resistant, such as cedar or redwood, or treated lumber. A pergola is top-heavy, so it must be sturdily built, employing standard construction practices. Proper footings are essential. Like a deck, it is exposed to harsh weather and must be maintained to ensure long life.

GROWTH OPPORTUNITIES

After you've decided on the arbor, trellis, or pergola you want to buy or build, you can start selecting the vines and plants to grow on the structure. Conversely, if you know what kind of vine or plant you want, you can decide which kind of structure will work best.

Many vines and roses are suitable. You'll find information on a selection of the most popular and reliable types in chapter 3. To make an informed decision among the choices, you should first understand how vines grow. In the wild, vines clamber everywhere, attaching themselves to trees or anything else they can, eventually assuming the shape of whatever they cover. But not all vines climb in the same way.

How a vine climbs will determine what kind of structure you must have to support it.

Vines or roses grow in four general ways.

■ **Twining.** These types of vines wrap themselves around vertical objects such as posts, chain-link fences, arbors, wire or string, and lattice. Morning glory and wisteria are two of the best-known twining vines. Do not let twining vines grow on live trees; they can kill a tree by strangulation.

■ **Clinging rootlets.** Ivy is the best example of this type of climber. It can be seen covering the sides of buildings or the outfield walls of Wrigley Field, the famous Major League Baseball stadium in Chicago. Creeping fig, wintercreeper, and climbing hydrangea are other examples. Clinging rootlets have suction discs or aerial rootlets that attach themselves to almost any surface that's not slick, including rocks and brick or stone walls. They grow horizontally, also. However, they are not good choices for growing on trellises or arbors. They become quite dense, and the only way to prune or thin them is to remove them from the structure.

■ **Tendrils.** Like expert knot-tiers, these vines reach out and attach themselves to objects, using modified stems called tendrils. Grape, sweet pea, and

▶ Clematis climbs over a simple arbor that marks the path to a hammock in the garden. The arbor's narrow top and sides are ideal for vines with tendrils.

▲ Several types of vines, including clematis, ramble up and over this pergola, providing beautiful blooms and cooling shade.

▲ Trained on a lattice trellis, roses create a dense, colorful, and fragrant screen in the landscape.

passionflower are some examples of vines that use tendrils. Some vines, such as clematis, have modified leaves, as well as stems, that act as tendrils. Like the twiners, vines with tendrils climb best on narrow, vertical surfaces such as fences, wire, or lattice, and they'll also invade other plants, such as shrubs or trees.

■ **Sprawlers.** Also known as climbers, these vines have long, lax stems and tend to sprawl. Even though they are called climbers, they have no mechanism to attach themselves to supports and must be tied to or handwoven through a material such as lattice. Bougainvillea and climbing and rambling roses are the best examples of sprawling plants.

▲ Rambling roses sprawl along a fence and climb up a trellis, but not without help. You must tie or otherwise attach them to the supporting structure.

QUICK CLIMBERS

Waiting several seasons for perennial vines to become established can seem like an eternity.

Granted, the results of waiting are well worth it when you finally see your trellis overflowing with supersize clematis flowers or when your arbor is engulfed in the fragrance and splendor of roses in bloom.

But you can get quicker coverage with annual vines. While the results aren't immediate, they are quick: In a matter of just weeks you can plant some seeds in the ground and cover a trellis, arbor, or pergola with vines that grow and flower profusely in one summer. Like their perennial cousins, these vines can add colorful blooms and texture to your landscape. They can also solve problems by screening out unsightly views or protecting an area against sun and wind. As a bonus, they create a habitat for birds and butterflies.

Morning glories are the annual vine most people recognize, but many others also are worth growing. Because they are so inexpensive (a packet of seeds might run you a few dollars) and grow so fast, they are great for getting kids interested in gardening. Some annual vines will grow right up the trunk of a tree and provide

blooms until frost. Some smaller vines will grow in pots with trellises attached, so they can serve as portable view-blockers in front of almost any unsightly element in your yard.

You can sow most annual vine seeds directly in the garden a week or two after the average last frost date. Keep the soil moist until the seeds begin to grow. Most like full sun and good, well-drained soil. The best time to fertilize annual vines is just as they begin to bloom. Frost will kill an annual vine, so after the season is over, pull the vines down and compost them. In warmer climates, some annual vines will grow year-round. Combinations of annual vines can be charming, such as sweet pea with morning glory, or canary vine with nasturtium or hyacinth bean.

▲ Nasturtiums climb up and hide the fence while creating a colorful backdrop for the flower bed.

◄ Bamboo poles against a fence make a great trellis for annual vines.

FIND YOUR INSPIRATION

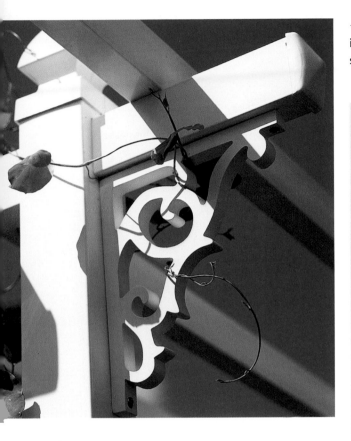

◀ A climbing vine finds plenty of footholds as it winds up a post and through fancy scrollwork.

ANNUAL VINES TO GRACE YOUR STRUCTURE

Sweet pea, morning glory, and moonflower are three of the most common annual vines. For more about these dependable plants, see the list of climbers in chapter 3. Other annual vines to consider include:

■ Balloon vine, which covers a trellis or pergola quickly to give you shade or a screen. It grows to 10 feet and has tiny white flowers, then greenish fruits.

■ Cup-and-saucer vine, a prolific vine that can grow to more than 20 feet in one season. Its peculiar 2-inch flowers look like fluted cups in a saucerlike calyx.

■ Twining snapdragon, named for its snapdragon-like 1-inch flowers in pink, blue, white, or red. It grows 6–12 feet. Grow in full sun.

■ Nasturtium, an old-fashioned flower that grows to about 6 feet. It is a beautiful companion to other vines with its spurred yellow, orange, red, and white flowers.

■ Canary bird vine, a nasturtium relative that has small featherlike yellow flowers and delicate leaves. All nasturtiums grow and bloom best in poor soil.

■ Scarlet runner bean, a vine that grows up to 15 feet, producing edible beans and scarlet flowers that attract hummingbirds. Grow in full sun.

■ Black-eyed Susan vine can be trained onto a trellis, but it's best used where its thin stems can dangle in the wind. It likes well-drained soil and full sun.

■ Hyacinth bean or Egyptian bean, with blue-green leaves that complement the vine's striking dark purple flowers and purple pods. A white one is also available.

■ Mandevilla, with large dark leaves and a large pink bloom. It's great for a deck or patio planter and is hardy enough to be a perennial in some warmer zones.

▼ Morning glory, a twining vine, climbs thin wires in a fanciful trellis that resembles a window.

CLIMBING ROSES

Like a setting in a romantic movie, an arbor overflowing with climbing roses can be a real showstopper in your yard. Traditional, country, or contemporary—climbing roses look great in almost any style setting. (The roses don't actually climb; they sprawl. You have to tie them to support structures.)

To get those beautiful blooms, experienced gardeners prefer to plant climbing roses as bare-root plants.

A bare-root rose looks anything but beautiful. But this awkward assemblage of stubby, thorny canes and wiry roots grows quickly. Look for dormant plants with roots swaddled in plastic in garden centers or nursery catalogs. Bare-root roses settle in with a minimum of transplant shock and quickly start to produce flowers.

Before you begin to plant the roses, however, decide where you want to plant them and what will support them. During the growing season, roses need at least six hours of sunlight. The soil should be fertile and well-drained. If you want the roses to spill over a trellis or arbor or ramble along a fence, for example, make sure the structure is accessible for pruning and can support the full-grown vine.

When you get your bare-root roses, plant them right away, following the steps on the next page. If you can't plant a bare-root rose right away, keep its roots moist and cool. (An alternative to a bare-root rose, a container-grown or potted rose can be planted any time it's available. Potted roses offer a convenient way to extend the planting season.)

▲ Rambling roses in full bloom add romance to the entrance to a shady pergola.

FIND YOUR INSPIRATION

◀ Pink climbing roses go over the top and peek out between the rafters of this pergola.

Planting

■ **Refresh the roots in water.** An hour-long soak (overnight, at most) plumps up shriveled roots. Add B vitamins (available at garden centers) to the water to help the plant overcome transplant shock.

■ **Clip off damaged roots.** Shorten roots that are too long to fit into the planting hole without bending. Some rose sellers trim the stems, or canes, for you. If they do not, remove the broken ends of canes, canes with blackened or diseased spots, and twiggy growth.

■ **Timing is crucial.** Plant bare-root roses in early spring before their leaves unfurl. Where temperatures reliably stay above 20 degrees, winter planting is best.

■ **Dig a generous planting hole.** Make the hole 12 to 18 inches deep and 2 feet wide, to give the roots growing room. Center a low mound of soil in the bottom of the hole. Position the roots on top of the mounded soil,

keeping the bud union (the knobby area where roots join canes on grafted roses) 1 to 2 inches above ground level in mild-winter areas; 1 to 2 inches below soil level in cold-winter areas.

■ **Fill and water.** Backfill the hole halfway with enriched soil. Slowly pour in the B-vitamin-enriched water in which you soaked the roots. Let the water saturate the soil. Fill the planting hole. Water again, using a hose.

■ **Build a shallow levee of soil** around the perimeter of the planting hole to collect water over the roots. Moats are unnecessary in a rainy region such as the Pacific Northwest.

■ **Cut off** all but three to five healthy canes. Prune the canes to about the same length at an outward-facing, 45-degree angle just above a bud to promote new growth. Keep the center open for air circulation. Don't worry about making a mistake; it's hard to go wrong.

▼ Prolific rose blooms engulf a rustic fence and clamber over the top of an arbor.

ESPALIER

▲ The popular espalier style palmette verrier resembles a candelabra. Training and pruning are best begun at planting.

▲ Several apple trees are grown side by side to make this Belgian fence espalier pattern.

WHAT TO ESPALIER

According to the North Carolina Cooperative Extension Service, these 20 plants are the best candidates for espalier. Check with your local extension office to see which plants might work best in your area.

- Apple, Crabapple
- Burford Holly
- Camellia
- Chinese Photinia
- Cotoneaster
- Fig
- Flowering Quince
- Forsythia
- Japanese Maple
- Korean Stewartia

- Pfitzer Juniper
- Pyracantha
- Redbud
- Sasanqua
- Southern Magnolia
- Star Magnolia
- Viburnum
- Winged Euonymus
- Winter Jasmine
- Yew

No discussion about training plant growth would be complete without mentioning espalier. A French word derived from an Italian word, espalier roughly translates to "shoulder support." The technique, in which trees, typically fruit trees, are grown against flat walls, was developed centuries ago in Europe as a space-saving measure. Today, gardeners espalier shrubs and woody vines as well as trees. Besides its space-saving benefit, many gardeners use espalier to express their artistic side.

To espalier, prune a plant, such as an apple tree, so that it has one main vertical stem. Then train the side branches until they achieve the desired shape. Choosing to espalier is a long-term obligation: Depending on the type of plant, the process could require several years of regular pruning and training. For example, it could take up to seven years for an espaliered apple tree to finally start producing the desired amount of fruit. Once the espalier is in the shape you want, it requires minimal pruning to keep its shape.

You can espalier a plant on any flat wall, as long as there is enough light and there is room in the ground for the plant. You can sometimes grow the espaliered plant in a container. Plants that work best are those with naturally spreading branches, such as apple, pear, quince, and camellia. Look for plants that are suited to your area and that already have a start on the branching pattern you want.

To support the plant, run three horizontal wires between nails driven into the wall or into

▼ This apple tree has been formed into a three-dimensional sculpture using espalier techniques.

posts that have been set in the ground. Use heavy-gauge wire and stretch it taut so that it can resist the pull of the branches as they try to grow toward the sun. Plant the tree, shrub, or vine 1 foot in front of the structure that will support it, and make sure at least two strong branches run in the same direction as the wires. It's best to train a tree against a south-facing wall that gets ample sun and a little afternoon shade.

Remove all but two shoots on each branch and attach those shoots to the wire with soft ties or stretchy tie tape that won't damage the bark. As the trunk grows, keep removing side shoots. When the trunk reaches the next wire up, allow two new side shoots to develop and attach them to the wire. As the shoots grow, you can turn the branches upward to create a candelabra pattern, as shown above, or keep the branches growing horizontally along the wire. For a more creative espalier, grow several plants and train them into a Belgian fence pattern, as shown opposite, top.

▲ An espalier trained in a candelabra pattern creates a point of interest on this wall. The lattice trellis highlights the espalier too.

TRADITIONAL

▲ This arbor's traditional style with a modern flavor perfectly complements many gardens.

Crisp, symmetrical lines govern traditional garden design. The simplest layouts are often the most elegant. Lush but uncluttered plantings with few and subtle color changes are hallmarks of this style. Often, a formal garden is divided into four beds (planted identically or very similarly) that are arranged geometrically around a central focal point, such as a statue, fountain, or birdbath. Other architectural elements, such as stately trellises and arbors, play a major role in this timeless look. Position them throughout to draw the eye upward.

The functional parts of a traditional garden include paths, structures, benches, and containers. Choose materials for these elements based on their durability, versatility, and architectural capacity. Concrete, brick, and native stone are good choices for pathways. Encourage the growth of moss for that ageless look of understated elegance. Concrete and cast iron are good choices for furniture and containers. They can sit outside through the toughest winter weather. Time-honored terra-cotta pots should be brought in at the end of the season where temperatures dip below freezing.

◄ Clean lines and traditional details make this trellis an attractive garden addition.

Metal trellises and arbors stand up well to the rigors of harsh winters. If you prefer the look of wood, consider structures made of naturally rot-resistant species, such as redwood and cedar. These softwoods also acquire an attractive, silvery patina over time. But cold, wet weather will eventually take its toll on any wood, so check arbors, pergolas, and trellises each spring for weak spots or wear, and make repairs.

For aesthetics, use a showy planting such as a clematis in front of a trellis to create a vertical focal point. A climbing hybrid tea rose or one of the old ramblers is a natural performer in the traditional garden and can turn an otherwise ho-hum arbor into a feast for the eyes and nose.

▲ This prefabricated metal arbor has the look of a Victorian garden accessory, but without the elaborate details.

◄ Plants growing on obelisks accent the entrance to this arbor, which is home to various plants in containers.

COTTAGE

Romance is always in the air in a cottage garden. For storybook charm, fill curving cottage garden beds to overflowing with colorful, fragrant plants.

There are no special design rules to follow, but as you plan your cottage garden, remember that half of its success will stem from what is unseen. Tuck a gurgling fountain or pond into a shady secret garden so that it is heard before it can be seen. Enhance the sense of mystery by incorporating secluded nooks into the plan and offering only glimpses of the landscape, rather than spacious vistas. Reinforce the cottage theme with latticework trellises and lush vines for privacy. Aim for a simple, charming, and captivating look.

In a cottage garden, abundance reigns

supreme. Instead of formal hybrid tea roses, landscape roses and climbers ramble up and over round-top arbors and billow over fences. Old-fashioned vines such as sweet pea and moonflower are almost a requirement. Combine

▶ Simple ladder trellises against the wall are just right for this lush cottage garden.

vines with clumps of tall plants such as hollyhocks, phlox, and larkspur and midsize daisies, zinnias, and coneflowers to form an unruly tapestry. Search flea markets for interesting containers, antique ornaments, and unusual artifacts to add an element of surprise to the cottage garden.

Cobblestone and brick work well for paths and circular or irregularly shaped patios. Many cottage gardeners cultivate low-growing plants that don't mind being trod upon, such as mint, for barefoot comfort along pathways. Place wood and metal benches with soft cushions in garden crannies. A tiny table for two with simple folding chairs can transform a quiet garden corner into an open-air cafe. Extend your enjoyment of the garden into the evening by setting votive candles in vintage canning jars.

▲ A romantic garden gate and a rose-covered arbor complete the cottage look.

◄ An arbor built from salvaged architectural pieces gives the look of a garden that has gone wild and grown over a building.

CONTEMPORARY

I f you want a beautiful but undemanding garden style, the contemporary paradise delivers. Pea gravel or a combination of gravel and pavers make easily maintained floors for contemporary outdoor rooms. It's a sophisticated, uptown look that requires only an occasional raking or sweeping. Create an outdoor version of a parquet floor by planting a creeper in the spaces between concrete pavers laid in a grid pattern. Maintain the path with occasional watering and mowing. If you want to have a patch of lawn, keep it small or consider alternatives to high-maintenance turf grasses. Buffalo grass, heathers, sedums, sempervivums, and creeping herbs are excellent groundcovers.

Mass plantings of easy-care ornamental grasses steal the show in the contemporary garden. Fill in the scene with tough-as-nails plants that have seasonal staying power, including herbs, yucca, daylilies, coreopsis, hostas, and ferns. For height and privacy, plant climbing hydrangeas, ivy, or other perennial vines.

Look for furniture that suits your budget and preferences. Everything from Adirondack chairs to sleek plastic and metal chairs will fit into the contemporary landscape. If you plan to entertain family and friends, place a roomy, casual dining table and comfortable chairs in a part of the yard accessible from your home. Arrange other chairs near traffic areas for after-dinner lounging or to supervise adjacent children's play areas. Ease the transition from garden to deck with hassle-free potted charmers such as Alberta spruce and geraniums. Use shredded bark mulch for low-traffic pathways.

◀ **Unadorned posts support a vine-covered pergola over an airy, contemporary-style patio. The outdoor fireplace provides a focus.**

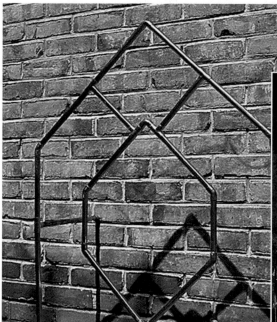

▲ A geometric copper-tubing trellis is just right for adding a contemporary touch.

▶ Steel hoop arbors and a pergola frame draped with canvas create a contemporary-style outdoor dining room.

Trellises, arbors, and pergolas with plain lines and little ornamentation work best in contemporary settings. A variety of finishes are suitable for structures with a contemporary or industrial look: enamel or clear finishes over wood or metal, rusted steel or patinaed metals, and unfinished treated lumber.

◀ Reinforcing mesh for concrete and standard lumber bolted together make a no-nonsense, industrial-look arbor for this urban garden.

RUSTIC

For a real back-to-nature experience in the garden, go rustic. Rustic gardens share the plants and freewheeling design philosophies of cottage and country gardens. However, they tend to take on a look all their own with one-of-a-kind structures spun from cast-off woods. A pergola crafted from willow twigs, for example, can appear to be rooted in place—a welcoming oasis of shade on a sizzling summer afternoon. With a string of white lights, it can become a romantic hideaway for an evening picnic.

■ **Whether made of rebar *right* or branches *below,* rustic arbors must look crude but be sturdy enough to support the plants.**

Any gardener can master the informal art of transforming scrap logs, branches, tree prunings, driftwood, and saplings into useful forms. Acquiring the raw material for a trellis, fence, or other rustic accent is easy. Comb local beaches or riverbanks for driftwood. Stroll through any wooded area after a windstorm to gather fallen branches. You may be able to get limbs from trees being cut down or trimmed for construction if you ask the contractor. Utility or tree service crews will often let you have some cuttings for free. Of course, you can use trimmings from your yard.

The longest-lasting woods for rustic structures include cedar, juniper, arborvitae, bamboo, second-growth willow, and some varieties of locust. Woods with shorter life spans (one season or two) include elm, wild cherry, mulberry, and ash. Grapevine works well for trellises, but it will only last a season or two.

Design rustic structures by first considering wood as a natural art form. Let each limb inspire your design: A soft crook in a branch can be a peak for an arch, and topsy-turvy twigs can fit together to form brackets and joints. Branches with crotches make great posts with built-in braces. Start with a smaller project, such as a window box or a short, straight trellis, to practice your skills and build up your confidence. Fasten larger pieces together with nails or screws. Lash smaller twigs and branches with twine or, for old-time authenticity, vines.

Arches and curves require pliable wood. Young wood is the most flexible. Bend twigs as soon as possible after cutting; after two or three days, the wood will likely break instead of bend. Attach twigs and branches with drywall nails and reinforce connections with wire. Green wood shrinks, so tighten wires with pliers a few weeks after building your work of art.

▲ A trellis made of twigs laced together adds charm to the garden with or without plants growing on it.

◄ Careful selection of branches is a key to success in building a complex rustic structure such as this pergola. Corresponding members should be roughly the same size and shape for the best-looking result.

VARIATIONS ON A THEME

▲ A pretty white porch swing turns this simple arbor into a place you want to visit.

Relaxation stations

Your arbor or pergola can have more than just good looks. You can make it into a desirable destination—a relaxation station—by adding a swing, built-in seating, or even a hammock. That's all it takes to create a comfortable setting for reading, napping, or just watching the world go by.

As you look at the arbors and pergolas shown throughout this chapter and those in chapter 2, consider ways to construct a relaxing structure for your yard. Even the projects that don't include seating areas or swings could be modified to include them. Use your imagination to create a structure where you can escape the summer heat and enjoy the simple pleasures of breezes, shade, and utter tranquility.

Today's outdoor living spaces are much more than just a spot in the yard for grilling hot dogs. They are a part of our lifestyle, extending our family rooms into the outdoors to take advantage of nature, sun, and fresh air. Here are some other ideas for making your outdoor living spaces more relaxing.

■ **Turn a terrace into a destination.** Rather than spending money to tear out a concrete slab and refill it with topsoil, consider building a pergola over the slab. This will make the area into an open-air pavilion with dappled sunlight that's delightful for entertaining. You can make it as shady as you like by adding climbing plants or topping the structure with fabric.

■ **Personalize your spaces.** You're much more likely to use an outdoor room if it includes elements you like, such as your favorite colors or furnishings. Shop around for art pieces, such as a birdbath or statuary, that capture your interest. These pieces will make the outdoor spaces your own.

■ **Match your home's style.** Be sure to match your outdoor retreat's design to the house's architectural style and the garden's style. For example, a southwestern-style courtyard goes better with an adobe home than would a formal English garden. Use your house's trim color in the outdoor decor to tie the spaces together. Consider the view of the yard from the

▲ **Comfortable chairs hang from the rafters of the deck-topping pergola above.**

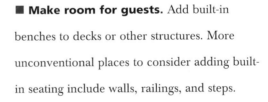

sitting space and think about how the outdoor space will look from inside the house.

■ **Consider the elements.** Nothing ruins the pleasure of sitting outside more than relentless, hot sunshine. A pergola ensures the outdoor room can be used any time of day. You can add shade by growing grapevines, roses, or other climbing plants over the top to form a living roof. With good planning, you can make yourself comfortable and your space usable year-round by addressing the impact of insects, sun, and humidity on your outdoor area.

■ **Create privacy.** Think of creative ways to use fences, structures, and plants to add personality and privacy to your outdoor relaxation area.

■ **Make room for guests.** Add built-in benches to decks or other structures. More unconventional places to consider adding built-in seating include walls, railings, and steps.

■ Built-in seating in the pergola *above* invites guests, while the swing *below* is cozy for two.

ENTRY STRUCTURES

▲ Roses ramble over the top of this gable-topped cedar gate, which embellishes the home's entry.

▶ This sturdy gated arbor clearly defines the transition between two areas of the garden. Climbing plants soften the structure's edges.

Whether it's the doorway to your front sidewalk or a gate that leads to a beautiful garden, an entry structure creates a grand first impression while enhancing your landscape.

An entry arbor establishes a border or limit to an area while providing a friendly portal for visitors. Some entry structures have gates that provide some security but are still welcoming.

When choosing a gate design, you can either complement or contrast the site. Consider durability as well as decorative details in a gate for a high-traffic area, such as a main entrance. Wrought iron will provide long wear and low maintenance, while wood will probably require periodic repainting or refinishing. Hang a gate on a sturdy, securely anchored post using weatherproof hardware. Install self-closing hinges or another type of closer along with a self-latching lock for convenience.

Front-door entry structures can add function as well as style to your yard. Rather than having a utilitarian, straight-line sidewalk to your door, you can have an attractive winding path of brick, stone, or gravel through the structure, ending at your front steps. On the way, visitors can be treated to a self-guided tour of a welcoming garden.

Enhance a typical 4-foot-wide path by flanking it with layered plantings. Place low-growing specimens next to the path, then step back with taller plants. If an entry path also leads to an adjoining space such as a

▲ A simple arbor offers a warm and friendly welcome to guests arriving at the home.

Make sure materials and construction complement your home's architecture, especially when built near your house. Take care to keep the structure in scale with the house and yard. When planning a gate, consider its impact on such things as newspaper and mail delivery. Municipal codes may require a specific type of enclosure and gate for a pool, pond, or spa.

▼ This substantial gate and arbor offer passage into the yard while maintaining privacy.

side yard, distinguish public areas from private ones with a gate or door. Creeping plants can grow between pavers or stepping-stones to fill the spaces with color. Certain kinds of plants such as creeping mint can also provide a sensory experience for visitors, releasing a pleasant aroma when crushed underfoot.

Outdoor lighting along pathways from entry structures will help guide people after dark. Modestly priced, low-voltage models are easy to install; or you can hire an electrician to install line-voltage lighting.

SCREENS

▼ Three lattice screens, the taller middle one topped with a playful gable, make a wonderful backdrop for this private seating area.

In an ideal world, backyards and gardens would be private sanctuaries to escape the rigors of daily life—places to relax away from prying eyes. Too often, however, nearby houses are so close that our private hideaways are the neighbors' views, and basking in your backyard can be like living under a microscope.

Building a wall or a solid fence is one way to block views, but such structures could keep you from enjoying cooling breezes in your yard. Screens, however, provide privacy while creating the perfect backdrop for patio and garden areas.

Less restrictive than a solid wall, a screen will let breezes pass through but still limit views. When built with lattice, screens are essentially large trellises. They can be freestanding or attached to other structures for stability. Training climbing plants to grow on a screen will create a living wall that will further shield your yard from uninvited eyes.

Lattice is inexpensive and demands no special skills to build— you can install it with only simple hand tools and an electric drill/driver. The term latticework refers to any decorative pattern made with narrow, thin strips of wood. Latticework designed to give privacy has 1½-inch openings; garden-spaced lattice has 3-inch openings.

Most lumberyards and home centers sell prefabricated 4×8-foot lattice panels for less than the cost of the lath to build one. These panels are easy to install because the cutting and nailing already has been done. Inspect prefab latticework carefully

▲ Climbers scramble up this garden screen. The lattice also supports a wall fountain.

before you buy, however. Cheaper varieties often are made with lath much thinner than that sold in individual pieces, and the staples holding cheap lattice together may be thin and dislodge easily.

▼ Here a pair of trellis grids screen a potting area from the main garden. The vines on the grids will hide the potting area further as they grow.

▲ This screen helps make the area with the water garden into a separate attraction.

STAND-ALONE PLANT SUPPORTS

Not all supports for climbing plants are as elegant as a formal arbor nor as impressive as a long, tunnel-like pergola. Some are quite humble. And they tend to have funny names, such as obelisk or tuteur. Others have names that are very utilitarian, such as vine pole or the ever-slighted beanpole.

Many gardeners agree: There are not enough of these simple plant supports in the world. Do your part by building a beanpole or vine pole (or obelisk or tuteur) in your garden.

▼ Vines will engulf the twiggy teepee below, which is known as a willow tuteur.

Four freestanding plant supports

■ **Obelisk.** This simple pyramid is every bit as functional as it is fanciful (shown on page 47). Without anything growing on it, this pointed garden structure is a handsome sculpture. For vines with stems that wind upward, push seeds into the ground around the base. For plants that have tendrils, tack fishing line onto the bottom slats and peaks for the vines to wrap themselves around as they grow upward.

■ **Tuteur.** The word is French for *guide and instruct*. This twiggy teepee guides vines to grow vertically until they finally engulf it. Typically built from willow branches, you could fashion a tuteur from branches of locust, fruit, or cedar trees. Wrap heavy wire around the top and weave willow rods through the sides.

■ **Beanpole.** A central post, its end buried in the ground, is surrounded by a base structure in this vertical gardening favorite. Strands of heavy string connect the top of the pole to the base on all sides. Bean vines, which would otherwise sprawl on the ground, instead grow neatly up the strings, conserving space in the garden.

■ **Vine pole.** Much like the beanpole in function, a vine pole has crossbars instead of string for the vines to grow on. Once this pole is engulfed in blooming vines, it looks like a column of flowers.

◄ Grow more than just beans on beanpoles. Morning glories, moonflowers, or other annual vines with bright blooms look great when intertwined with the beans.

▲ This black-eyed Susan vine, like other annuals grown from seed, eagerly grows up a vine pole.

► Bamboo rods lashed together to form a three-dimensional grid create a smart solution for supporting top-heavy flowers.

Starting Point

By now, you may be ready to add one or more garden structures to your yard. But first you need to consider how such a structure will fit into the overall scheme of your landscape. For that, you'll need a plan.

If you are an experienced gardener, you may already have a landscape plan in place and know exactly where to place these structures. If you don't, you'll need to take inventory of what your yard offers. A surveyor, landscape architect, or landscape designer can help you

chart out your yard, usually for a fee. You also can do the measuring and sketching yourself.

Go out to the yard with a notebook, the longest measuring tape you have, and a pen or pencil. First, make a rough sketch of your property's layout. Next, carefully measure property lines, then locate the house on your drawing by measuring from each corner perpendicular to the two nearest property lines. Finally, measure and mark all the other structures and the trees and plantings you plan to keep. Put the figures on your rough sketch as you go. At some point you'll want to mark the eaves, first-floor doors and windows, downspouts, meter locations, relevant utility and water lines, and anything else that may affect your plans. Check local building codes, deed restrictions, and setback and easement regulations early in your planning. Accurate measurements count for more than neatness at this point. Also note on your map where the yard level changes and where water drains, if you know. Then transfer your measurements and locations of landmarks onto graph paper. This is your base plan.

Rather than repeatedly drawing the base plan, lay tracing paper over it to sketch ideas on. You can scribble, erase,

▼ **Draw bubbles on a scaled plan of your yard to show areas for various activities and functions. Indicate places that may need screening. This helps you decide where to put structures.**

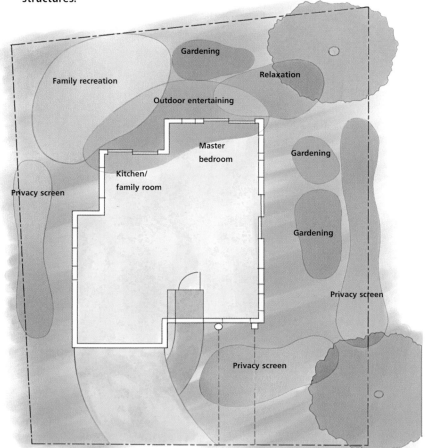

Gardening

Relaxation

Family recreation

Outdoor entertaining

Master bedroom

Gardening

Kitchen/ family room

Privacy screen

Gardening

Privacy screen

Privacy screen

draw, make notes, or replace the sheet with new tracing paper as your ideas percolate. At first, instead of sketching specific ideas on the tracing paper, simply draw bubbles representing the possible general uses for each area of the yard: entry, outdoor living, service, and so on. Most of the front and perhaps some of the side, for example, could be the entry area. Most of the back and perhaps part of a side yard could be reserved for outdoor living and entertaining. Decide early on whether you'd like to adopt a single landscape style, such as formal, natural, English cottage, or another. This saves you time and helps you develop a more unified design. It will also help you decide what kinds of structures to include. Cut out some smaller

◀ This arbor looks like it belongs because it mimics the arch over the home's front door.

bubbles from any kind of slightly thicker paper to represent areas that will have a specific use, such as a patio, pergola, deck, arbor, or pool. Move these patterns around, trying different arrangements within the broader space. Also set aside space for a service area or two. These areas in your landscape will accommodate everything from trash cans, boats, and clotheslines to pets and firewood.

■ Not all landscape structures have to be pricey or new. If you have a puckish nature, grow climbers on trashy treasures from the attic or garage, such as the ladder, *left*, and headboard, *above*,

PLANNING AND DESIGN

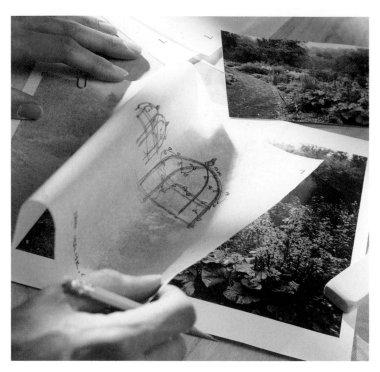

▲ To help visualize a structure in your garden, draw the proposed project on tracing paper laid over a photograph of your landscape.

Put these service areas in the least conspicuous but most convenient spots available. As you sketch the bubbles and begin to draw more specific ideas, double-check all dimensions to be sure the pieces you're considering will fit. Refer, too, to any lists you made of your family's outdoor needs. Frequently check what the rest of the family thinks about the plan. Concentrate on problems and solutions at this stage, not fine detail. Think of the plants as architectural forms: background or specimen trees, high or low screens. Save the decisions about which varieties to plant for later.

Remember that your paper plan is accurate, but flat. Walk around the yard and pace off proposed changes. Sit on a step and visualize the finished scene in three dimensions. Lay out

hoses to indicate the edges of patios. Put up sheets to mark the height of fences or arbors. For quick elevation views, which will help you visualize even better, enlarge photos of your house and yard, lay tracing paper over them, then sketch in the planned changes.

Make additions to your landscape only with a specific purpose in mind—whether it's to solve one of your yard's problems or to accent one of its best features. Start gathering ideas by observing the good and bad points of other yards in your neighborhood. Notice details: colors and textures of flowers and foliage, interesting paths or a charming gate, or the way an entrance planting distinguishes one house from the others around it. Browse through books, magazines, and Internet sites.

Some experts suggest that you wait a year and observe your yard through all seasons before you dig into any major work. If you don't mind waiting, spend the year compiling a list of dislikes about your setting: lack of privacy or outdoor living space, too much wind, or too little light, for example. Good landscaping can solve most, if not all, of your yard's shortcomings. Also think of how things will look not just when the work is completed but 5, 10, even 25 years from now.

Another thing to consider is maintenance. Although installation is done only once, maintenance goes on forever. A lawn, for

◀ The window is the focal point of this wall, and the trellis wrapping around it adds a harmonious design element plus color when the vines bloom.

■ Obelisks, *left* and *far left*, are bold garden accents. One is simple and the other more ornamental, but both serve the same function—supporting growing vines.

example, takes more time, expense, and natural resources, such as water, than any other landscaping option. To simplify the landscape, cut your lawn down to a workable size with areas of groundcovers or mulches around trees and shrubs. Put in a rose garden if you love to work at that or a vegetable patch or orchard, but avoid such landscaping features if you just don't have the time. Arbors, pergolas, trellises, patios, decks, walks, and permanent plantings require little maintenance work and expense after the initial construction. In return, they give plenty of outdoor living enjoyment for each

dollar spent. Throughout the process, you may want to consult a landscape professional–a landscape architect, landscape designer, or landscape contractor–for help.

■ Landscape architects are the planning experts, comparable to a building architect in training. A landscape architect can most help you while the property is being designed. Although landscape architects do mostly commercial work, many will consult with homeowners on an hourly basis, and some will oversee entire residential landscaping jobs.

PLANNING AND DESIGN (CONTINUED)

▲ **A good eye for design is needed to create a beautifully detailed arbor like this. The details, along with the curved framing members and a light, might make building it a job for a professional too.**

Because of their expertise, landscape architects tend to be the most expensive landscaping professionals.

■ **Landscape designers** often do much the same work as landscape architects, but they have less training and usually are more plant oriented. The fees of landscape designers employed by nurseries are often absorbed if you buy enough plants from the nurseries.

■ **Landscape contractors** employ crews that will perform the actual labor of installing your landscape. If you hire a landscape contractor, be sure to talk about what materials you are expected to provide and ask for samples of any materials the contractor will supply.

■ **Before choosing a landscape professional,** ask the owners of yards you admire for recommendations. Or call four or five landscapers listed in the phone book and ask for addresses where you can see their work. Then go out for a look. Keep doing this until you've found at least three professionals who do high-quality work, then ask them for bids on your job. Depending on your own time and expertise and your site's complexity, you may not need a professional. But the money spent to consult an expert—especially concerning such problems as difficult grading, sliding hillsides, or high walls and decks—is usually worth the satisfaction of a job done right, and safely. Remember, however, that no professional can know your needs and dreams like you can. That's why your good

▶ **Converting old architectural trim into a trellis and setting it in the garden can be a simple and fun family project.**

planning becomes even more important when you are putting the results into the hands of a highly paid person.

■ **Work carefully:** Be especially careful with existing trees and topsoil when planning and working on your landscape. Once lost, both take many years to replace. During construction, protect your trees from machinery. Transplant small, choice shrubs and trees that stand in the way. Protect your soil from being compacted. Before building or making major changes in grade, scrape the topsoil and pile it separately; you can ensure good planting soil by spreading the topsoil over the finished surface.

▶ Simple trellises on the porch posts are easy to build and install. Climbing roses will add color to the front of the house.

SHOPPING FOR A STRUCTURE

I f you don't want to build them yourself, you can buy trellises and arbors at home centers, garden centers, specialty garden shops, crafts festivals, and from catalogs and Internet retailers. (Some assembly may be required.) Trellises, which tend to be smaller than arbors or pergolas, are the most readily available. Some are works of art, with woven twigs or forged metal. Just attach them to a wall or push them into the soil and wrap the plants around them as they grow. Ready-made steel and wood trellises are shown above.

Arbors are available in wood, plastic, and metal. Even rather large, architecturally significant arbors and pergolas can be purchased and shipped from specialty retailers, though they can be expensive. If you buy a complex kit, you still might need to hire a contractor to assemble your structure if you're not handy.

FOR YOUR COMFORT

Many factors will affect the comfort of your outdoor living spaces. Get them right, and you'll be happy for years to come. Miscalculate, and you could end up with a lovely garden feature that you hate to visit.

To achieve the results you want and avoid landscaping mistakes, consider the characteristics of each part of your yard. How much sun does an area get? Is a certain spot more like a wind tunnel than a side yard? Is that low spot in the backyard reminiscent of a marsh after it rains? Would you prefer some

▼ **The addition of lattice panels, a comfy garden bench, and potted plants makes this arbor an inviting destination.**

▲ **This pergola shades the back door of the house and provides a cool place to relax on hot, sunny days.**

shade on the path to your restful arbor with a porch swing?

As part of your landscape planning, keep track of how many hours of sunlight each area of your property receives. If an area gets six hours or more of direct sunlight, it is considered a sunny area. Areas that receive less than six hours are considered shady.

There are several degrees of shade, ranging from light (the least shady) to dense (areas that receive little sun). An area of partial shade receives about four hours of sun a day, either directly or indirectly. When you are making your landscape plan, mark areas of sun and

◄ It would be difficult to pass by this arbor without stopping to relax on the swing. The arbor incorporates turned porch posts, lattice, and old-fashioned fancy millwork.

shade, the degree of shade, and how many hours of sun fall in each area on your base map.

Repeat this observation during each season and note the changing angle of the sun. Because the sun is much lower in the sky in winter than in summer, some areas that are shaded in summer may be sunny in winter, or vice versa. Make a note of areas where you'll want to augment or reduce shade seasonally.

Note where trees provide shade and where buildings cast shadows. These areas might make good spots for a summertime retreat or a bed of shade-loving plantings. A spot that gets full sun may be perfect for a large play area with just grass. A pergola over a pathway could provide the cool corridor you need to block the blazing midsummer sun. You might be able to use trellises to transform a blank garage wall from a giant reflecting oven to a soft and colorful (even artistic) display of full-sun climbing roses.

By planning carefully you're more likely to make decisions about your yard that will provide the level of comfort you seek.

▲ A pergola provides a restful retreat just outside the home's front door. Screens on the sides enclose the structure, adding a contemporary element to contrast with the classic columns.

CHAPTER HIGHLIGHTS

PRESENTING 30 TRELLIS, ARBOR, AND

PERGOLA STRUCTURES YOU CAN

BUILD YOURSELF. HERE'S A BREAKDOWN:

TRELLIS, ARBOR, AND PERGOLA PROJECTS

Chapter 1 showed how garden structures can improve your yard. This chapter gets down to the nuts and bolts (and nails and wood) of building trellises, arbors, and pergolas.

Here you'll learn exactly how a particular outdoor project goes together, complete with plans, detailed illustrations, and step-by-step instructions that will guide you through the construction process. Some projects require only a few basic hand tools and no building experience. Others call for a few handheld power tools and more do-it-yourself skills and experience. A few will appeal mainly to an experienced amateur or professional woodworker with a full complement of shop tools. Don't be discouraged if you come across an unfamiliar tool, technique, or material. You'll find answers to your construction questions in chapter 4, "Building Basics," which starts on page 128.

SIMPLE TRELLISES

Anyone can build a trellis. In fact, many trellises can be built with only a few hand tools. A case in point is the inverted tripod shown at *left*.

■ Garden tripods are traditional supports for clematis and other vines. Turn one on its head to make a nontraditional tornado-shaped support. You can assemble it in minutes with perennial supports and stakes–things you might already have in the garage. Uncovered, it's not a thing of beauty, but a fast-growing vine will soon hide the hardware and become an inverted cone of foliage and flowers. At the end of the growing season, the trellis disappears into the garage just as easily as it went up in spring.

■ Construct the trellis from three sizes of round wire grids—the kind used to support peonies and other floppy perennials—minus their legs. The three 8-foot-long stakes are plastic-coated metal tubing. Plunge each stake 2 feet into the ground for stability. Lash the grids to the stakes with twist ties. (See illustration A, *opposite*.)

■ Illustrations B and C show two other easy ways to give plants a leg up. Staple plastic bird netting to a wall, fence, or other vertical surface (illustration B). Staple the netting loosely so that climbers get a good grip.

■ A trellis can be as simple as a bamboo stake driven into the ground (illustration C). Here again, twist ties hold vines in place.

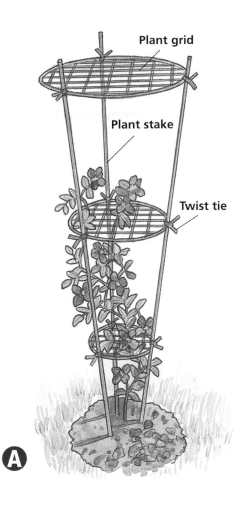

Plant grid

Plant stake

Twist tie

A

PROPAGATING CLEMATIS

Your one clematis vine can become two if you bury one of the shoots and stake it in place. Nicking the shoot with a knife and wrapping it with a wad of sphagnum before burial often helps roots form. After a few months, give the new vine a tug to see if it has established itself. If it has, snip the shoot from the mother plant and transplant it.

■ If you plant your clematis below the soil line, roots will stay protected and moist. And if you start a new vine, you can let the vine and roots become long and sturdy before transplanting it.

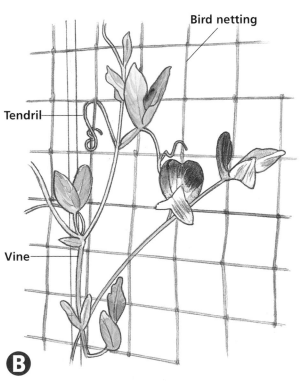

Bird netting

Tendril

Vine

B

Bamboo stake

Twist tie

C

ROSE CAGE

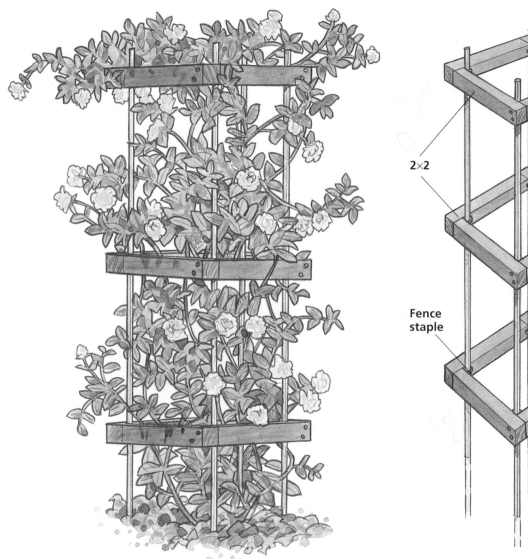

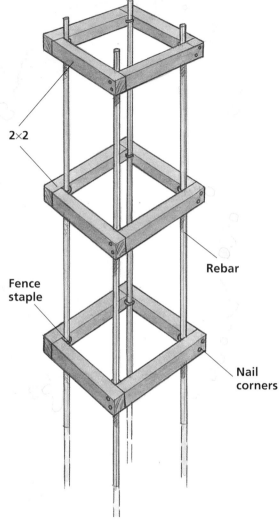

2×2

Rebar

Fence staple

Nail corners

Everything comes up roses inside a trellis like this one, and you can build it with just a handsaw, hammer, and staple tacker. For the legs, you'll need four concrete reinforcing rods (rebar) cut to the length you want. (Allow an extra 12 inches of length to sink below the ground surface.) Here's how to build the trellis.

1 To make the wooden frames, cut pieces of 2×2 lumber 12 to 14 inches long. Drill pilot holes for nails to minimize splitting and nail the brackets together into square frames with 8d galvanized nails.

2 Stand the brackets up on edge on a workbench or other flat surface, spacing them about a foot apart. Position the first reinforcing rod in the inside bottom corners of the frames and staple the rod to each frame. Secure the second rod in the same way. Flip the trellis over and position and secure the remaining rods.

3 Sink the trellis into the ground around a climbing rosebush or other vining plant and watch it grow. Once you discover how easy this trellis is to build, you'll probably want to make some more of them.

SIMPLE TRELLISES

ROSE POST

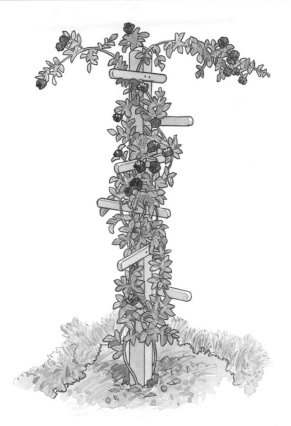

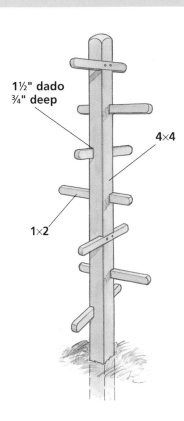

1½" dado
¾" deep

4×4

1×2

This climbing post calls for a bit more carpentry skill and helps vining plants reach for the sky. It consists of a 4×4 post with 1×2 rungs. Make the climbing post any height you prefer but be sure to add enough length to sink it below the frost line.

1 Round off the top of the 4×4 with a rasp or surface-forming tool to help shed water. Next, cut seven 2×2s 12 to 14 inches long and round off the ends of each piece. Or leave them square, if you like.

2 On the post, lay out dadoes spaced 12 inches apart for the rungs. Cut the dadoes with a router or saw and chisel. Fasten the rungs to the post with 8d galvanized nails. (If you don't want to cut notches, just nail the rungs to the post.)

3 Dig a hole and set the post on gravel as shown on page 164. The post doesn't support anything other than the rungs, so you don't need to set it in concrete.

THE READY-MADE OPTION

The easiest way to put a trellis in your garden is to purchase a ready-made one at a garden center or home store. Made of wood, metal, or vinyl (which can't rot and never needs painting), these come in traditional trellis configurations, such as lattice and fan shapes, that you can use as is or as part of a larger structure you build yourself. Later in this chapter, you'll find several projects that could include ready-made trellises. Shop carefully to avoid flimsy construction that will likely fall apart in just a few years.

CORNER AND STEEL ROD

Bring greenery to a corner or any other tight location with this easy-to-erect structure. All you need to build it are 2×4s, 1×3s, cup hooks, and string, wire, or chicken wire for the plants to hang on to. For ease of construction, nail the trellis together first, then plant it in the ground. Except for the time it takes for the finish to dry, you can do the entire job in an afternoon.

1 Cut two 2×4 posts (A) to the height you want, plus enough extra length to reach below the frost line in your region.

2 Cut two more 2×4s 24 inches long to serve as top and bottom rails (B). Nail or screw the rails to the posts with butt joints.

3 Cut four 1×3s 29 inches long for trim (C). Nail these to each side of the rails and posts as shown in the detail drawing *below.*

4 Sand, prime, and paint the wood, or apply clear finish. (To learn about choosing finishes, see page 170.)

5 Cut reinforcing mesh or chicken wire to size. Screw cup hooks in place, spaced to support the mesh.

6 Dig holes for the uprights, tip your trellis into them, plumb and brace it, and pack earth around the posts as explained on page 164. A structure this light doesn't need concrete footings.

CORNER TRELLIS

ASSEMBLY

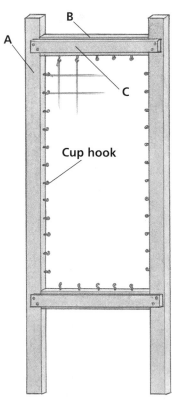

Cup hook

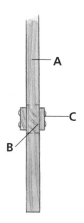

STEEL ROD TRELLIS

This trellis serves as a 6-foot-high fence that can divide one part of your yard from another. It also can provide privacy from the street or neighbors. The plants climb steel rods or dowels ¼ inch in diameter. Build the trellis/fence in sections about 30 inches wide.

❶ Set 4×4 posts (A) as shown on pages 162–164. For durability, set the end posts in concrete, and the others in earth.

❷ Cut four lengths of 2×2 for rails (B, C) to fit each space between posts.

❸ Drill ¼-inch holes through the top and bottom rails (B); drill alternate through holes and ¾-inch-deep blind holes in the middle rails where shown.

❹ Cut one 2×4 to serve as the bottom rail (D) for each section. Toenail these to the posts.

❺ Nail the rail (B) with five holes to the bottom rail (D). Toenail the lower center rail (C) to the posts, the blind holes facing up.

❻ Thread rods down through the holes, then place the other center rail (C) on top of them, with the rods going into the blind holes.

ASSEMBLY

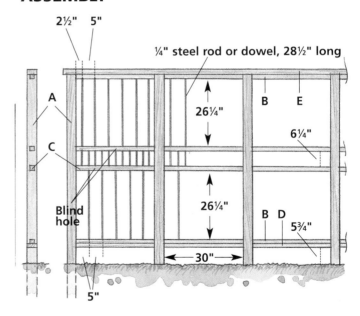

❼ Nail the rail (B) with six holes between the tops of the posts. Thread the rods down through the holes into the blind holes in the bottom center rail (C).

❽ Cut a 2×4 for cap rail (E) long enough to span all the sections of your fence. Nail it, flat side up, to the tops of the posts.

FAN TRELLIS

This classic trellis is easiest to build if you have a tablesaw and drill press. Make it from redwood or cedar for a natural look.

Make the arm assembly and spreaders

1 Rip seven arms (A), each measuring $5/16 \times 1 1/8 \times 72$ inches, from 2×6 stock.

2 Stack the arms face-to-face. Bind them with masking tape, then drill three $7/16$-inch holes through them as shown in the Drilling the Arms illustration, *opposite*, spacingl the holes where marked. Drill two $1/4$-inch holes where shown.

3 Cut a threaded brass rod into two $2 5/8$-inch lengths with a hacksaw.

4 Remove enough strips of masking tape at the bottom end of the stacked arms so that you can spread glue.

5 Insert the threaded brass rods through the $1/4$-inch holes, position the washers, and tighten the acorn nuts. Clamp the assembly and remove excess glue with a damp rag. Let the assembly dry; remove remaining tape.

6 Rip two 36-inch lengths of stock to $3/8$ inch square. Bevel the corners to make the stock octagonal, as shown in the detail illustration *opposite*. Set one length aside for the top spreader (B). From the other, cut a piece $18 1/4$ inches long for the middle spreader (C) and a piece $7 9/16$ inches for the bottom spreader (D).

Assemble the trellis

1 Mark the center of each spreader, then insert the spreaders through the holes in the arm assembly. Fan the trellis arms and center spreaders B, C, and D in the middle arm. Drill pilot holes and drive a #18×$5/8$-inch solid brass escutcheon pin through the middle arm into each spreader.

2 Refer to the two-step Using the Spacer Block illustration, *opposite*, for directions on using the block to space the trellis arms on the top spreader. Fasten each arm to spreader B by repeating the drilling and nailing procedure explained in Step 1.

3 Attach the arms to the center spreader C. Use the $3/4$-inch dimension of the spacer block to gauge the position of the outermost arms, and nail them in place. Position the remaining arms by eye and fasten them to spreaders C and D.

4 Drive a 36-inch length of electrical conduit 20 inches into the ground. Attach the trellis to it with conduit straps.

EXPLODED VIEW

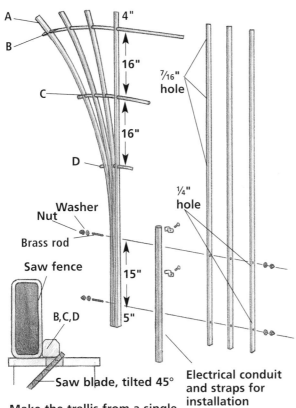

Make the trellis from a single 72" 2×6, ripped into strips.

DRILLING THE ARMS

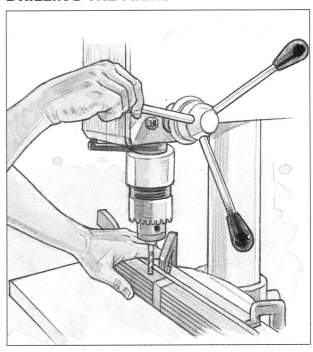

▲ Tape the arms face-to-face and join them together with masking tape at several locations. Mark center points for five holes where shown on the exploded view. Clamp the stack to the drill press fence and drill holes through the arms.

USING THE SPACER BLOCK

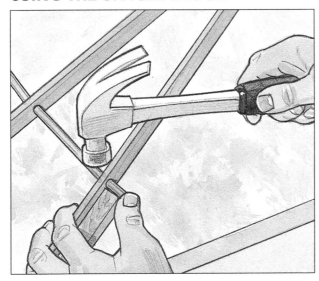

▲ Cut a piece of scrap $3/4 \times 3/4 \times 5^3/8$ inches. Use its $3/4$-inch dimension to determine the distance the spreaders protrude through the outermost arms, then drive #18×$5/8$-inch escutcheon pins through predrilled pilot holes.

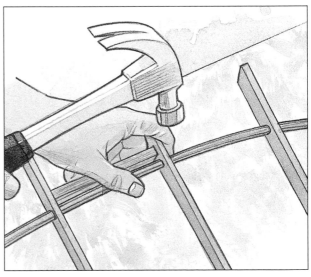

▲ Attach the center arm in the same way, then use the length of the spacer block to locate arms on both sides of the center arm. Secure these with escutcheon pins too.

ARCHED SCREEN

A trellis can provide a dramatic transition from one area of your yard to another, or it can provide privacy, especially when foliage fills in the blanks. This project does both, thanks to an arched portal surrounded by latticework. Here's what you'll need to build it: 4×4 posts, 2×4s for the frame, 1×1s for cleats (actual dimensions ³/₄×³/₄ inch), lattice, ³/₄- and ¹/₂-inch plywood, nails, some gravel, and dry-mix concrete. This project calls for power hand tools—a router, jigsaw, and circular saw (you can also use a handsaw)—and basic carpentry skills. To get an idea of what's involved, refer to the Cutaway View on the *opposite page*.

Start with the arch

1 For the arch, cut two semicircular arches from ³/₄-inch plywood. Each arch has an 18-inch outside radius and a 14¹/₂-inch inside radius.

Cut two more similar arches but extend the ends 4 inches past center. From ½-inch plywood, cut an arch with a 17½-inch outside radius and a 14½-inch inside radius. Nail and glue all arches together, placing the ¾-inch-thick arches with extended sides on the outsides and the ½-inch-thick arch in the center. The center arch is narrower to form a groove for the lattice.

2 Rout a ½×½-inch groove centered on the outer face of each 4×4 that forms the bottom part of the arch. These grooves also accommodate the lattice. Rout a ¾-inch deep, 4-inch-long section from opposite sides of the top of both of the 4×4s. Join the arch to the 4×4s, lining up the grooves and notches. Nail the extended legs of the arch to the posts.

Erecting the framework

Because this is a substantial structure, the posts should be set in concrete (see page 164). Add 2×4 framing and nail cleats to the inside of the frame as shown at *right.*

Nail prefab vinyl or wood lattice panels between the cleats as shown, or build your own latticework, as shown on page 160, and nail it in place.

Cutting arches in lattice

Cut the arch in the lattice as shown at *right.* First, make a cardboard template to match the shape of the arch. Mark the arch and reinforce the lattice along the curve. Then cut the lattice along the mark with a jigsaw or keyhole saw. You can use the same technique to cut any shape in the lattice. With wood, be sure to paint or stain raw edges that are exposed by the cutting.

Install the arch last, sliding its center groove over the lattice and attaching the arch to the frame with 2×4 blocking.

CUTAWAY VIEW

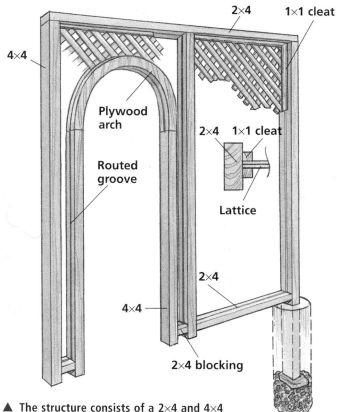

4×4

Plywood arch

Routed groove

2×4

1×1 cleat

2×4   1×1 cleat

Lattice

2×4

4×4

2×4 blocking

▲ The structure consists of a 2×4 and 4×4 framework into which lattice panels are inset. Make the arch with laminated plywood.

CUTTING THE ARCH

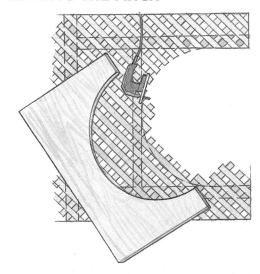

▲ Mark lattice for the arch cut with a cardboard template, above. Support the lattice with a framework before cutting.

PYRAMID TRELLIS

The French call this structure a *tuteur*, but "pyramid trellis" aptly describes it in English. By any name, this garden classic rises high to show off climbing plants such as the clematis shown here. You can construct it in an afternoon. Because it's not sunk into the ground, you can easily relocate this plant-loving pyramid whenever you like.

Figuring the angles

1 Start by cutting four 2×2 vertical members (A) to the length you like. (The ones shown are 8 feet long.) Overlap the ends of a pair of legs (A) to form a triangle. Adjust the angle until you're pleased with the triangle's proportions and saw through the two overlapped pieces to create the angles where they meet. Use these angles to mark and cut a second pair of legs.

2 Nail the pairs of legs together at the top, then determine the lengths of the four rungs on each side. Space them evenly along the legs. Cut the 1×2 rungs (B) to length. You'll need four each of the four different rung lengths.

3 Cut a dado 1½ inches wide by ⅜ inch deep in the center of each rung. Fasten a set of rungs to each of the pairs of legs (A) with 6d galvanized nails to create a pair of triangular ladders.

4 Cut four 1×2 stringers (C) to a length about 6 inches shorter than the vertical members. Lay them across the rungs and mark locations for dadoes that will fit into dadoes in the rungs, as shown in the Dado Detail drawing. Cut the dadoes and glue two of the stringers into the two triangular ladders. Nail them at the top.

Put it all together

1 You'll probably need someone to help brace the assembly while you nail the remaining rungs and stringers in place. To make the job easier, predrill holes in the rungs and hold a block behind the vertical members while you drive the nails through the rungs and into the vertical members. Or secure the rungs with galvanized screws.

2 Glue the final two stringers to the rungs and nail their tops to the vertical members.

3 For a rustic, natural look, leave the pyramid unfinished and let it weather. For a longer-lasting tuteur, apply paint or stain, following the instructions on pages 170–173. You'll find it easier to apply finish before final assembly.

DADO DETAIL

EXPLODED VIEW

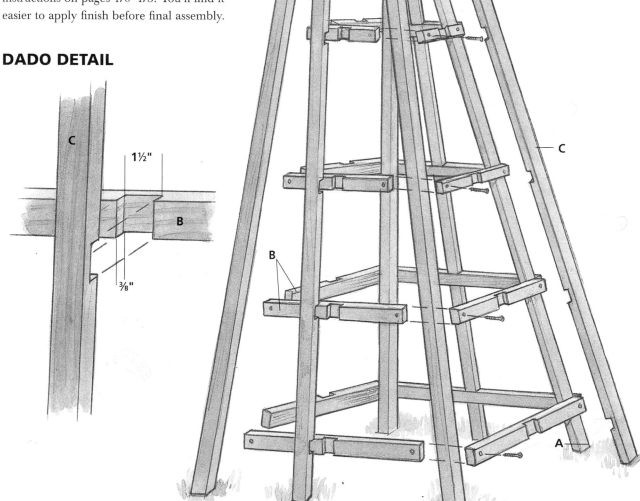

TRELLIS TRIO

Here is a fence that is not a fence, a screen that is not a screen, and a vine pole that is more than a vine pole. These trellises do the work of all three. Place them close together for maximum mass and privacy. Angle them like half-open shutters to soften a corner of your yard. Or put them in facing parallel rows to make an open-roof arbor.

Building the trellises

To build the three trellises, you'll need eight 2×4s 8' long, 16 1×2s 8' long, and for the arched top, two 2×10s 3' long.

1 Start construction by cutting a 30-degree angle at the top end of each 2×4 post (A). If you are making the arch-top trellis, cut the post tops square. A power mitersaw will make all cuts except the arched trellis top. Cut the two 1×2 cleats (B); nail each one to the inner face of each post, centering it side to side and with its top end 1½ inches from the top cut.

2 Make a point on the tip of each of the 1×2 trellis uprights (C) with 45-degree cuts. Cut the uprights to length. Crosscut the 1×2 trellis rails (D), then nail the rails and uprights together into a lattice assembly.

3 Cut the 2×4 top rail (E) to length; position it between the posts and drive deck screws into countersunk pilot holes. Nail the lattice assembly to the cleats (B).

4 Complete the assembly by cutting the top pieces (F) and screwing them into position. The illustrations on the *opposite page* show how to complete each top.

EXPLODED VIEW

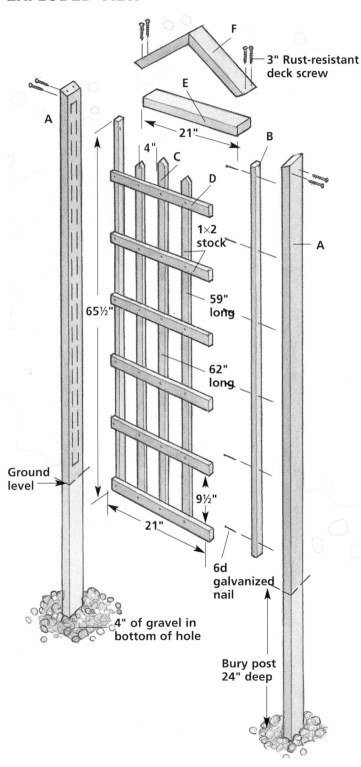

F

3" Rust-resistant deck screw

E

21"

4"

C

D

A

B

A

1×2 stock

65½"

59" long

62" long

9½"

21"

Ground level

6d galvanized nail

4" of gravel in bottom of hole

Bury post 24" deep

ARCH

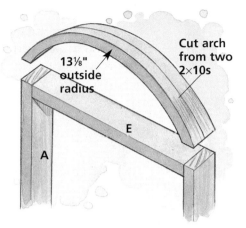

Cut arch from two 2×10s

13⅛" outside radius

E

A

▲ For the arch-top trellis, cut the post tops (A) square. To make the arch, laminate two 2×10s face-to-face and cut the arch with a jigsaw. Use nails and weatherproof carpenter's glue to join the 2×10s, and a string and pencil to draw the radius.

TRIANGLE TOP

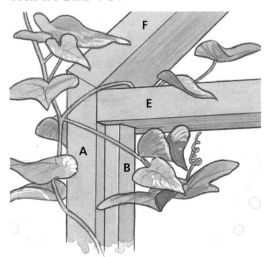

F

E

A

B

▲ For the triangle-top trellis, cut 2×4s with 30-degree beveled ends (F) and fasten them together as shown, with horizontal and vertical screws through and into the post tops (A).

GARAGE DOOR TRELLIS

Two-car garages—even structures for three or more cars—are commonplace these days, but all too often their big doors (or multiple doors) dominate the look of a home's exterior. To soften the appearance of your garage, consider stretching an overhead trellis across the door or doors. This one, painted to match the rest of the home's trim, juts out about 20 inches from the garage, 8 feet above the driveway.

Painting the parts before you assemble the unit is easier, with less risk of messing up doors and the driveway. Also, paint between joined surfaces improves their protection. Once you've encouraged vines to grow, it will be a long time before the trellis is painted again.

The trellis has Craftsman-style details, including beveled edges and decoratively cut ends. You could build one without those details for simplicity or to give it a different look. You can build it with one bracket per side or two, as shown *below*. If your garage has separate doors, you could put brackets between the doors too.

Start with the brackets

1 Each bracket consists of a 22-inch-long 2×6 girder (A) and a 2×4 knee brace (B). With a jigsaw, scrollsaw, or bandsaw, cut the corbeled ends of each girder to the dimensions shown. Also cut 1½-inch-wide dadoes ¾ inch deep where shown at the top of each girder. These will accommodate the beams that extend across the front of the garage.

FRONT VIEW

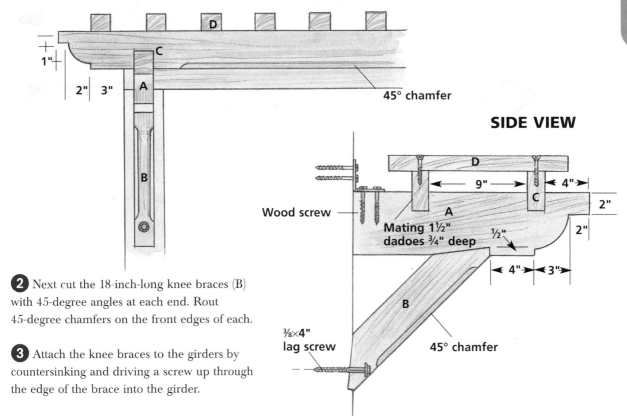

45° chamfer

SIDE VIEW

9"   4"

2"

Wood screw

Mating 1½"
dadoes ¾" deep

½"

2"

4"   3"

B

⅜×4"
lag screw

45° chamfer

2 Next cut the 18-inch-long knee braces (B) with 45-degree angles at each end. Rout 45-degree chamfers on the front edges of each.

3 Attach the knee braces to the girders by countersinking and driving a screw up through the edge of the brace into the girder.

Now mount the brackets

1 Drill and countersink holes for a ⅜-inch lag screw near the base of each knee brace. Have a helper hold each bracket in place, then drill holes through the braces into framing at each side of the door. Make sure the lag screw is long enough to go through the wall and securely into the framing. Install a suitable anchor if you are installing the trellis on brick or masonry.

2 Install a 3×3×3-inch galvanized metal L-bracket on top of each girder to attach the trellis to the wall. Affix the brackets to the girders with 3-inch wood screws. Be sure the screws penetrate into the wall framing or install suitable anchors in the garage wall.

Cut and install the beams

1 Make the two 2×4 beams (C) the width of your door plus the amount you want the trellis to overhang at the sides. (An overhang of 6 inches on each side is shown; it looks fine for a two-car-width garage door.)

2 For design interest, cut corbels at the ends of each beam like the ones on the ends of the

girders. Or leave the ends square for a different look. Also chamfer the lower front edge of each beam, if you like.

3 Cut 1½-inch-wide dadoes ¾ inch deep in each beam to mate with the dadoes in the girders. Set the beams in place and secure them with 8d galvanized nails driven through the tops of the beams into the girders.

Top off your trellis

1 Make 2×2 rungs 16 inches long (D) for the trellis. For the spacing shown in the illustrations, you'll need one rung for each 5 inches of the overall trellis width. (You may need to slightly adjust the rung spacing to keep it even.)

2 For an added decorative look, bevel the outer ends of the rungs to make points on them.

3 Nail the rungs to the beams with an 8d nail through each rung at each beam. Plant vines such as trumpet vine or morning glory and watch your garage grow a new look.

Garden Retreat

Supported by twin trellis towers, this sturdy bench provides a restful spot where you can watch your garden grow. You can even enjoy evenings outside, thanks to low-voltage uplights at the base of each trellis.

Build the trellises

1 Using a tablesaw, radial-arm saw, or circular saw, cut eight 2×4 posts (A) to length. Make them long enough to stand about 6 feet tall above the ground. Rout a chamfer across one corner of each board ¼ inch wide where shown in the exploded view. Glue and nail a 2×2 cleat (B) to each post.

2 Miter-cut eight 1×8×19½-inch top members (C), then rout a ½-inch cove along the bottom edge of each. Do the same with eight 1×6×19½-inch members (D), routing a cove along the top edge of each. Glue and nail the top and bottom members to the posts.

Set the posts

Set and plumb the posts as shown on page 163. For a lasting installation, set them in concrete.

Install lattice panels

1 Make your own lattice panels (see page 160) or purchase prefab panels at a home store.

2 Nail lattice panels (E) to the inside surfaces of the 2×2 cleats (B) on three sides of each tower. In the two corners where the lattice panels meet, glue and nail 1×1 corner cleats (F) to the lattice panels, as shown in the exploded view. In the remaining two corners, attach the 1×1 cleats so that there is enough space to slide a panel between the 2×2 and 1×1 cleats. The resulting slots allow you to raise each lattice end panel for access to the lights. Slide the end panels into place.

Top off the trellises

1 Miter-cut the moldings (G), then glue and nail them to the 1×8 top members (C). For the caps (H), miter four 1×6×27-inch pieces and round over the top and bottom edges with a ⅛-inch round-over bit; glue, clamp, then use finishing nails in the corners to form a square.

EXPLODED VIEW

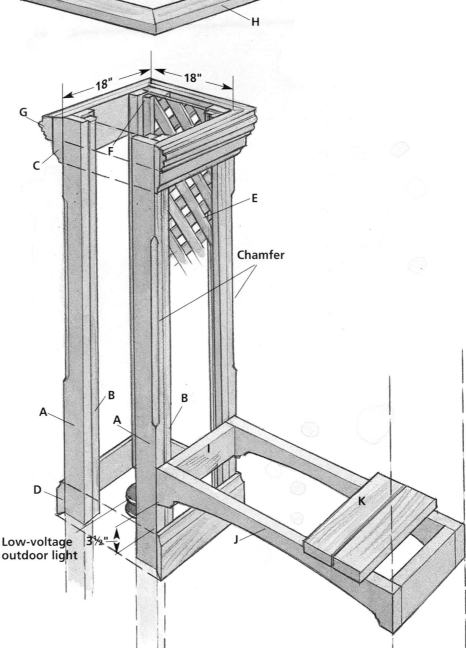

To keep the cap secure on the trellis tower, miter four 12-inch 2×2s to fit inside the tower; glue, clamp, then use finishing nails in the corners to form a square. Nail to the bottom of the cap.

Install the bench

1 Drill pilot holes in the 2×6×14-inch bench frame ends (I). Screw the ends to the trellis towers. Cut a pair of 2×6×45½-inch frame sides (J).

2 With a jigsaw, cut a curve with a 38-foot radius along the bottom edge of each side (J), then rout ½-inch coves at each end of each radius. Drill pilot holes and screw the sides to the end pieces.

3 Cut eight 2×6×18-inch bench slats (K) and nail them to the side frames, spacing the slats ⅛ inch apart for drainage.

Install the lights

1 Mount the lights according to the manufacturer's instructions. Many have stakes you simply stick into the ground.

2 Run wires from the lights to a transformer plugged into a grounded 120-volt outdoor receptacle. For added romance and intrigue, fit the lights with colored lenses.

▲ You'll need intermediate woodworking skills and a few power tools to build this structure. Construct the trellis towers first, then sling the bench between them. Everything goes together easily with standard-dimension lumber and lattice panels, which you can make yourself or purchase prefabricated.

CIRCLE-TOP TRELLIS

Topped with a quartet of circles, this trellis brings distinction and dimension to a blank exterior wall. Or modify it to fit on a fence. It's really not as complex as it looks once you see how these elements go together.

Start with the frame

1 Cut 2×2 frame stiles (A) to length for the trellis height you prefer.

2 Cut the $^3/_4$×$^3/_4$-inch lattice crosspieces (B) and uprights (C) to the length you prefer. For the trellis shown, with four circles $11^1/_4$ inches in diameter separated by three $^3/_4$-inch-wide lattice stiles, make the crosspieces $47^1/_4$ inches long. Cut the uprights the same height as the stiles (A). Glue and nail $^3/_4$×$^3/_4$×$1^1/_4$-inch support blocks (D) to the stiles, spacing them 12 inches from center to center.

3 Lay out the frame pieces on a flat surface and square them up. Glue and nail or staple the crosspieces (B) into place. Glue and nail or staple the uprights (C) to the crosspieces.

Make the circles

1 Edge-glue two 8-foot lengths of 1×8 together to create blanks for the circles. When the glue dries, cut the blanks into eight $11^1/_4$-inch-long pieces. Using a scrollsaw or handheld jigsaw, cut the blanks into circles that have a $5^5/_8$-inch outside radius and a $4^1/_8$-inch inside radius. Drill a hole as an entry point for cutting the insides of the circles.

2 Use exterior-grade weatherproof wood glue to laminate pairs of circles face-to-face. Glue and nail the circles into position between the lattice strips at the top of the trellis framework.

Install the trellis

Prime and paint the assembly, apply an exterior clear finish, or leave it natural to weather gray. Mount the trellis to the side of your house with hinges at the bottom and hooks at the top. This allows you to fold the trellis out of the way when the house needs to be cleaned or painted.

MARKING CIRCLES

Squares and straightedges are great for straight lines, but they can't throw the kind of curves you need for a project such as the trellis shown here. What you need to use depends on how big the circle must be and how much accuracy you need. The drawings below show three ways to proceed.

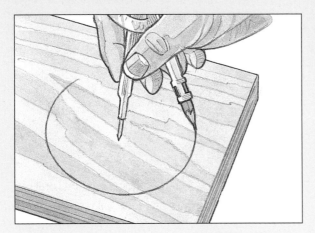

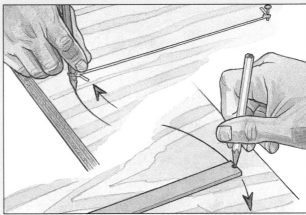

To mark small circles, a simple compass, like the one you probably used in school, will do the job. Mark a spot at the center of the hole and set the compass width to one-half the diameter of the circle. For accuracy, clamp the compass tightly in position and hold it as perpendicular to the surface as possible.

If your compass isn't large enough for the circle you want, make your own compass out of a pencil, brad, and string. For greater accuracy, make a notch at the end of a strip of wood. Nail the strip in place with a brad at the center of the circle. The notch holds the pencil in place for a smooth, accurate line.

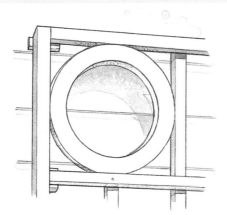

▲ Circles inset into lattice squares bring geometric interest to any trellis. Spacing the trellis several inches away from the wall creates shadow patterns that change throughout the day.

▶ You can build this trellis in a weekend with basic woodworking skills and tools. Alter the plan to fit your site, if needed.

ASSEMBLY

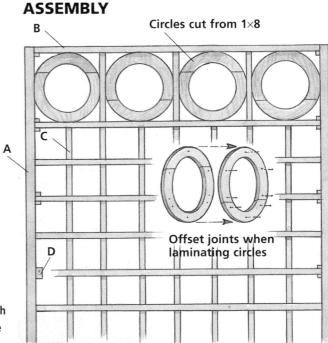

Circles cut from 1×8

B

A

C

D

Offset joints when laminating circles

GATED ARBORS

Garden gates have their own way of saying, "My world and welcome to it." Your garden gate, like your garden, also says something about you. As you can see by the character of these three arbors, a garden gate does not have to say, "Keep out."

A gated arbor can be freestanding–a pause along a verdant path. Most, however, serve as portals through fencing or a wall that embraces all or part of a yard. For a country garden effect, locate fencing and a gated arbor at or near your front property line. (Check your community's building codes for any mandated setback.) Or construct a gated arbor in a side yard or backyard, where it can serve as a transition from one planting area to another.

SEE-THROUGH SIMPLICITY

◄ This picketed classic has a gate you can look over and through. The illustration shows how it goes together. For more about constructing an arch-top arbor, see pages 78–81.

CRAFTSMAN CANOPY

◄ A Craftsman-influenced gated arbor of redwood or cedar welcomes its owners home every evening. Study the illustration, then check out pages 82–83 for more about building a square-top arbor.

DOORWAY TO PARADISE

◀ To build the arched top for the door and arbor, refer to pages 78–79. Use prefab lattice for the fence and window, or make your own as shown on pages160-161.

▲ For more privacy, build a tall solid-board fence and hang a harmonizing door in the arbor. A round window in the door provides a tantalizing peek at what's beyond. Plants can grow on the fence and arch.

BUILD AND HANG A GATE TO LAST

A gate that's strong and true will give you years of trouble-free service. Hang the gate before you attach fence screening so you can correct an out-of-square opening.

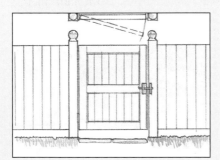

Plumb the posts and square the opening. Make the gate ½ inch narrower than the opening.

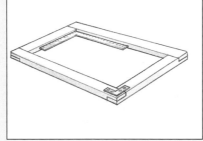

Use butt or lapped joints at corners of the frame. Square the frame before securing the corners.

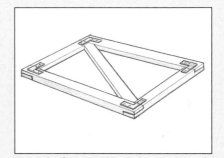

Brace the frame with a diagonal piece of wood that runs from the top of the hinge side to the bottom of the latch side.

Screw or bolt the hinges to the gate and prop it in the opening. Fasten the hinges to the post.

Stop

With the gate closed, mark its inside edge on the latch post, then nail up a strip of wood to serve as a stop for the gate.

You can mount latches on the top or side of the gate. Three types are shown. The thumb latch (center) requires boring to install.

RUSTIC ARBORS

If you want an arbor that blends comfortably into a wooded setting, consider going beyond dimensional lumber and building a rustic log structure. You can buy cedar or redwood poles in a variety of diameters, adapt split-rail fence posts and rails, or—for a more organic look—fashion your arbor from saplings, tree trunks, and branches.

The rustic trio shown *below* supports climbing roses and twining clematis while defining the borders of a perennial garden. Low-voltage lighting strung from arbor to arbor provides twinkling nighttime interest.

The Exploded View, *opposite page*, shows how this style of arbor goes together. Adapt dimensions to suit your setting. Connect the pieces using one of these techniques:
■ Drill holes and use spikes, lag screws or carriage bolts, as shown on pages 146–147.

■ Notch the parts and fit them together log-cabin fashion, securing each joint with a spike or two.
■ Lash pieces to each other with copper wire, heavy-duty twine, or vines (for a rustic look).

Rustic arches

Supple twigs and branches, bent into arches and other decorative shapes, can bring yet another dimension to a rustic arbor. Willow and hickory are the most supple woods, but other species also bend easily. Don't let the material dry out before you try to bend it. For best results, work with pliable wood within 24 hours after it's cut.

Finally, just because the structure of a rustic arbor was recently a growing thing doesn't mean you can just stick it in the ground and expect it to remain standing for very long. Treat the bases of posts with wood preservative before setting them.

NATURAL-FIT ARBOR

The frame for this arbor consists of 4-inch-diameter cedar poles and peeled rhododendron cuttings. These natural materials merge inconspicuously with the vines they support, providing welcome shade for a winding garden path.

Bamboo—available in a variety of lengths and diameters—also works well for the horizontal parts of a rustic arbor. It's a poor choice for posts, though, because it rots when it's sunk into the ground.

EXPLODED VIEW

Use larger-diameter material for widely spaced top rungs, smaller material for closer spacing.

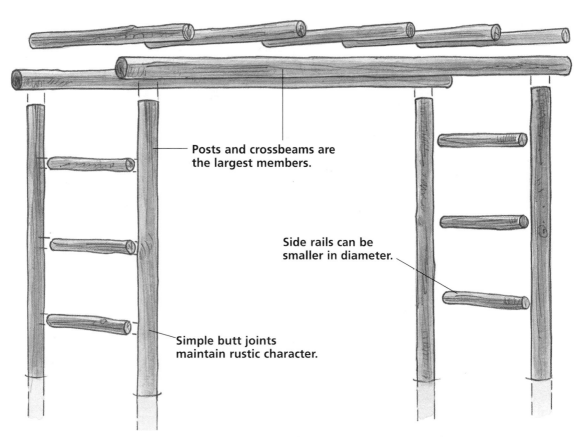

Posts and crossbeams are the largest members.

Side rails can be smaller in diameter.

Simple butt joints maintain rustic character.

Arched Arbor

This sturdy arbor makes a romantic entryway or practical divider for your landscaping plan. Once climbing flowers are established, it will be an eye-catching, softening feature. The overhead arch, cut from 2×8s, is easier to build than it might look. With 4×4s as the primary framing members, the arbor is substantial.

Building the arches

1 On a large piece of cardboard, draw a template for the arches, using a compass made from a nail, a string, and a pencil. With a framing square and protractor, divide the arch into four equal sections and cut out the four arch segments.

2 On the 2×8, use the cardboard segments to lay out the arch members. Cut them out with a jigsaw. Temporarily attach the arch sections together with 3×¾-inch mending plates.

Assembling the arbor

1 Dig the postholes below the frost line and shovel a little gravel into the bottom of each. Set the posts and temporarily brace them into position, checking for plumb in all directions. Starting with one post, mark a point 7 feet above the ground. Level across to the other posts and mark them. Use a square to draw a line around each post and cut it with a handsaw or circular saw.

2 Nail 2×4 horizontal braces to the tops of the posts, leaving 1½ inches at each end for the arches, as shown *opposite*. Position the arches, then attach the 4×4 horizontal braces, cut to the same length as the horizontal 2×4 braces. Install the 1×3 crosspieces, using a scrap of 1×3 as a spacer. When the arbor is assembled, gradually fill and tamp the holes.

ARCH LAYOUT

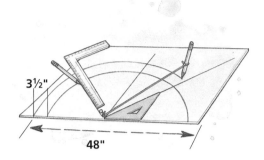

1 Make a cardboard template for the arches. The arch measures 3½ inches wide by 48 inches across. Lay out the arcs with a nail, string, and pencil. Divide the arch into four equal segments, using a framing square and 45-degree triangle as shown

CUTTING THE ARCH

2 Mark the arch segments on 2×8 lumber, then cut them out with a heavy-duty jigsaw. Splice the segments together with mending plates to create each arch. (You'll remove the mending plates after the arbor is assembled.) Allow room above and below the plates so you can nail through the arches into the crossbraces as you assemble the arbor.

ASSEMBLY

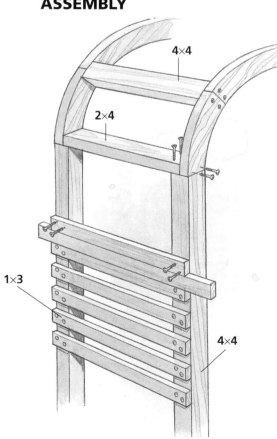

3 Set a pair of posts spaced 32 inches apart from outside face to outside face. Set a second pair of posts, similarly spaced, located 48 inches from the first pair. Plumb all the posts and temporarily brace them, as shown *below.*

SETTING POSTS

4 Connect each set of posts with 2×4 top braces as shown at *left.* Nail the arches to the braces and connect the arches with 4×4 braces at each splice. Screw 1×3 slats to the posts and arches.

Arched Arbor with a Seat

Start with the supports

1 To form the seat supports, cut three pieces $1\frac{1}{16} \times 3\frac{1}{2} \times 22\frac{1}{8}$ inches. Then cut the three backrest pieces $1\frac{1}{16} \times 3 \times 20\frac{1}{2}$ inches.

2 Using the Forming the Seat Support and Forming the Seat Backrest drawings on the *opposite page*, machine the supports and backrests for half-lap joints that will connect the bottom of the backrests to the rear of the seat supports.

3 Clamp the seat supports together and, using a jigsaw or bandsaw, cut all three to the seat contour.

4 Assemble the half-lap joints and glue the seat support/backrest assemblies together.

5 Cut the seat front rail and top rail to $1\frac{1}{16} \times 3 \times 41$ inches. Bevel-rip the front edge of the top rail at 15 degrees, as shown in the Slat Detail inset on the Side View drawing. Referring to the inset, rout $\frac{1}{8}$-inch round-overs, drill mounting holes, and screw the rails to the seat supports and seat backrests.

Now for the slats

1 Cut 24 seat slats $\frac{3}{4} \times 1\frac{3}{8} \times 41$ inches. Rout $\frac{1}{8}$-inch round-overs along the top edges of each. Then rout a $\frac{1}{2}$-inch round-over on the slat that will be the front edge of the seat.

2 Drill screw pilot holes and screw the slats to the seat supports and seat backrests. Space the slats $\frac{1}{4}$ inch apart as shown on the Slat detail of the Side View drawing.

A contoured seat turns an arched arbor–or any other arbor, for that matter–into a comfy place to watch your garden grow. Construct the arched frames first (see the previous pages), making each 41 inches wide between the legs on the inside. Install a 2×8 spreader between the arches in each side of the arbor, $11\frac{3}{4}$ inches above the ground. The seat side supports attach to these spreaders.

SIDE VIEW

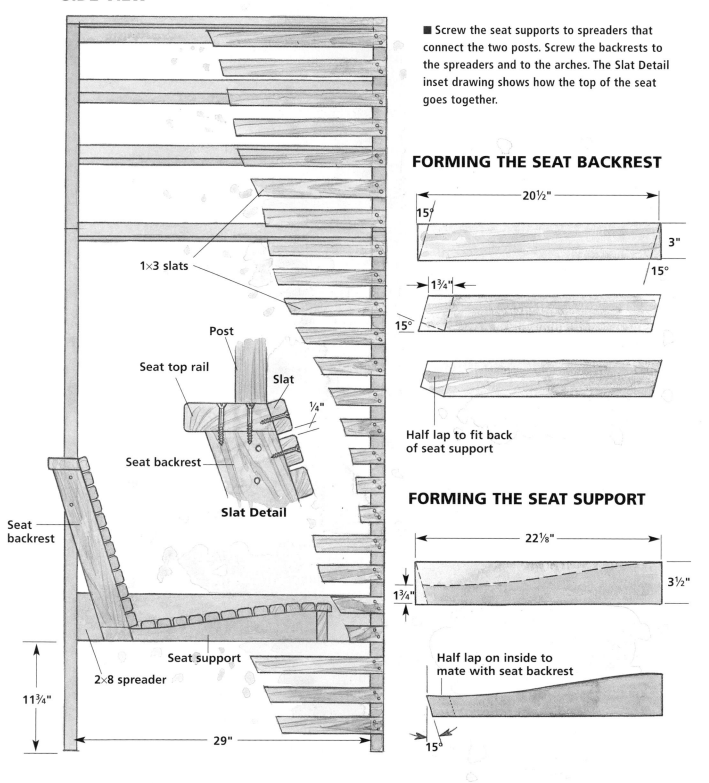

■ Screw the seat supports to spreaders that connect the two posts. Screw the backrests to the spreaders and to the arches. The Slat Detail inset drawing shows how the top of the seat goes together.

FORMING THE SEAT BACKREST

20½"

15°

3"

15°

1¾"

15°

Half lap to fit back of seat support

FORMING THE SEAT SUPPORT

22⅛"

1¾"

3½"

Half lap on inside to mate with seat backrest

15°

1×3 slats

Post

Seat top rail

Slat

¼"

Seat backrest

Slat Detail

Seat backrest

Seat support

2×8 spreader

11¾"

29"

SQUARE ARBOR

Have a sturdy stepladder on hand and get someone to help install the top pieces.

Getting ready

Dig the postholes and set the posts on the first weekend to allow time for the concrete to set and cure. To set the posts, dig postholes deeper than the frost line. Add 2 to 4 inches of gravel to the bottom of the holes and set the posts. Connect the posts with temporary bracing, check for plumb in all directions, and pour the concrete. Allow five days for the concrete to set and cure. Paint or treat the arbor pieces before you assemble them, perhaps while the concrete is curing.

Cut the rafter ends

1 Make a cardboard template for marking the 2×6s. Draw a rectangle 5½ inches wide and at least 17 inches long to represent the 2×6s. With a compass, draw arcs from the points shown on the drawing *opposite top*. Cut the template from the cardboard with a utility knife.

2 Trace the pattern from the template onto both ends of each rafter. Cut the rafter ends with a jigsaw or bandsaw.

Assemble the arbor

1 Cut all the posts level with each other, about 9½ feet above the ground. Attach the four lower rafters to the sides of the posts with 3-inch galvanized deck screws. Add 1×2 trim beneath each, using 6d finishing nails. Either butt the ends as shown on the *opposite page* or miter the corner joints.

Here's a solid portal topped with an elegant but easy-to-build roof. Heavy 6×6 posts set in concrete provide firm support for the specially cut flying rafters on top, making a substantial entryway or focal point for your landscape. While the most demanding task will be cutting the shaped ends of the flying rafters, a person with average carpentry skills can produce this impressive garden feature. Allow a couple of weekends for the project.

You will need a heavy-duty jigsaw or bandsaw to cut the curved ends of the 2×6s. To cut through the 6×6 posts, make the initial cuts with a circular saw, then finish with a handsaw.

② Lay out the upper rafters so that they are evenly spaced, and attach by predrilling pilot holes and driving 3-inch deck screws at an angle through the upper rafters into the lower ones. Top the structure off with 1×2s. Attach them with 1⅝-inch screws.

③ Nail 2×4 braces to the posts. Cut prefab lattice panels or make your own, as shown on page 160. The lattice should lap the braces evenly at the top and bottom. Attach it with 1¼-inch screws. On the inside of the arbor, attach 1×2 nailers with 1⅝-inch screws and screw the lattice to the nailers.

RAFTER ENDS

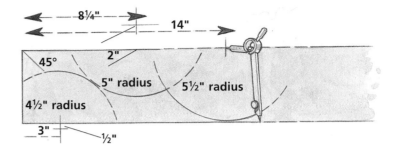

▲ To make a template for the rafters' shaped ends, draw a rectangle on cardboard the width of a 2x6. Mark points along its sides at the dimensions shown and use these as centerpoints for drawing arcs.

EXPLODED VIEW

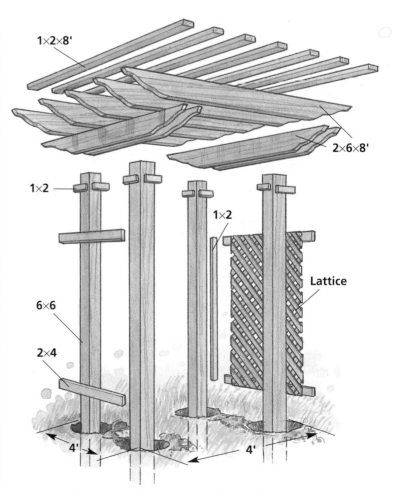

▲ Nine flying rafters—five up top and four below—give the arbor a pagoda look. To build it, you will need basic carpentry tools plus a heavy-duty jigsaw or bandsaw to cut the rafter ends.

SELECTING BANDSAW BLADES

You'll find bandsaw blades from ⅛ to ¾ inch wide. Narrower blades turn a tighter radius than wider blades. For accuracy, smoothness, and blade life, use the widest blade possible. A ¾-inch blade will work best for the gentle radii on this arbor's rafter ends.

Bandsaw blades generally range from 3 to 16 teeth per inch. Use a 3-tooth blade when cutting 2-inch-thick material, an 8-tooth blade for ¾-inch stock, and a 16-tooth blade for ¼-inch material. These recommendations leave 4 to 6 teeth in the material at one time.

TRIANGULAR ARBOR

Start with two basic frames

1 Prefabricate the framing by fastening notched top plates to each set of posts as shown in the drawing *opposite top.* Square the structures and add temporary crossbraces so that you can set the whole section into postholes at once. Set the sections in the holes, check that they're plumb, and secure them with four more temporary braces screwed to stakes. Pour concrete and trowel it so that it slants away from the posts, just above grade. (This keeps water from gathering at the base of the posts.) Allow five days for the concrete to cure.

Complete the structure

1 Add two more 2×4 top plates to tie the frames together, fastening them with 3-inch deck screws. Cut four 2×4 rafters $33^{15}/_{16}$ inches long with 45-degree cuts at both ends. Join the upper ends of the rafters with angled 3-inch deck screws. Set the triangle in place to check the fit. Adjust as needed and fasten to the top plate with 3-inch screws. Use $1^{5}/_{8}$-inch screws to attach the 1×3 slats to the posts and rafters. Maintain equal spacing between the slats.

The clean, spare lines of this arbor will fit into any part of your yard. Once the posts have been set, the rest of the structure can be built in a half day. Widely spaced 1×3 slats allow room for even the most robust climbing plants. You could space the slats more closely or cover the sides and roof with lattice, if you prefer.

SETTING POSTS

48"

▲ Assemble the frames and set them first. Notch the top plates and screw them to the tops of the uprights. Square the assemblies and brace them with temporary diagonal crossbraces. Plumb the frames with stakes and more braces.

ASSEMBLY

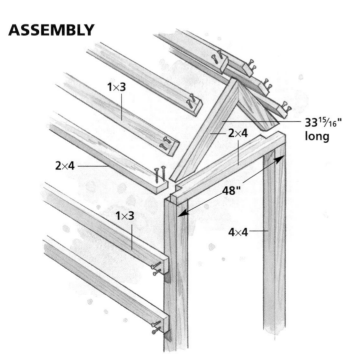

1×3

2×4

2×4

1×3

2×4

33¹⁵⁄₁₆" long

48"

4×4

▲ Join the frames with two 2×4 top plates. For the triangular ends, cut four 2×4 rafters 33¹⁵⁄₁₆ inches long, making 45-degree cuts at each end.

LANDSCAPE LESSONS

These tips may save you time and money as you lay out your yard.

■ Sure, it's sunny now, but will it be in three years? After a trellis or arbor is built and trees grow bigger, will you still have sunshine where you want it? That sunny wildflower patch beside the back fence might end up in shade if you plant trees or build structures nearby.

■ Sit at the kitchen table or in the study and look out at your landscape-to-be. What would you like to see? Plan views from inside looking out. Otherwise, you may end up seeing the back of a shrub or wall.

■ It's easy to assume that an arbor or other structure should go in the backyard, but it's a mistake to think that all of your great landscape ideas belong there. Plan schemes for the front and side yards, too, including benches, flower beds, arbors, and anything else you enjoy.

■ Paths usually should be at least 3 feet wide to allow two people to walk side by side. Allow extra space for plants to spill over the sides. It's okay to make some paths wide enough for only one person at a time, but also include wider paths or allow space for a bench along the side.

GARDEN GATE ARBOR

Nothing adds more to the allure (and privacy) of a backyard "secret garden" than a stately gate. Build this gate into a new fence or add it to an existing one. Either way, walking into your backyard will never be the same again.

Plant a pair of posts

1 Once you determine your gate's location, dig two holes 10 inches in diameter with their centers 50¾ inches apart. Set and brace 6×6 posts (A) in these holes as shown on pages 162–167. Trim the tops of the posts level with each other.

2 For the post caps, start by cutting two 1½×5½×5½-inch blanks for the cap tops (B) and two ¾×4½×4½-inch cap bases (C). Bevel the 1½-inch-thick caps where shown on the Post Cap drawing on page 88.

3 Glue and nail the cap bases, centered, to the cap tops, using exterior glue and 4d galvanized finishing nails. Drill countersunk shank holes through the caps where shown. Apply construction adhesive, position the caps, and drive in the screws.

Cut the parts for the overhead

1 Cut the 2×6 main joist (D, *next page*) to 76¼ inches long. Make the template for marking and trimming shown on page 88 and use it to mark the 3½-inch-radius cutouts on the joist ends where shown. Jigsaw close to the lines, then sand to the final profile.

2 Cut the six 2×6 cross joists (E) to 25½ inches long. Form the end cutouts in the same manner as those in the main joists.

3 Turn the cross joists upside down on a pair of sawhorses and clamp them together with their ends and top edges flush. Using a square, draw lines across the parts' bottom edges where dimensioned in the illustration on page 88. Adjust your portable circular saw to cut 2¼ inches deep. Guided by a straightedge clamped to the cross joists, make two cuts to define the notches' sides. Then cut a series of closely spaced kerfs through the waste between these two cuts. Finally, clean out the notches with a 1-inch chisel.

4 Sand and finish all your arbor parts with primer and two coats of exterior latex paint.

POST POSITION AND SURROUND ASSEMBLY

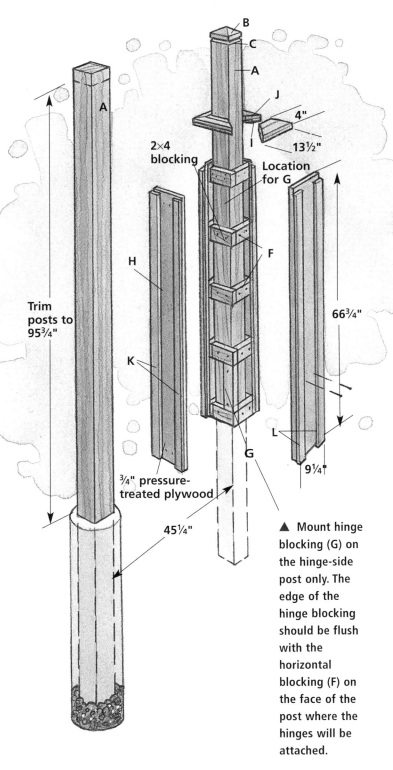

▲ Mount hinge blocking (G) on the hinge-side post only. The edge of the hinge blocking should be flush with the horizontal blocking (F) on the face of the post where the hinges will be attached.

GARDEN GATE ARBOR (CONTINUED)

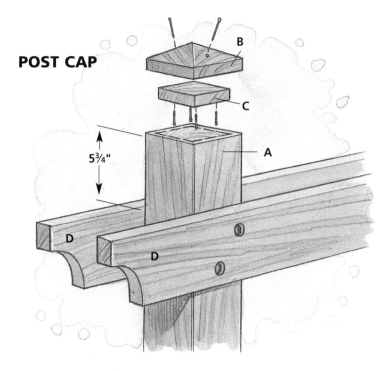

POST CAP

$5\frac{3}{4}$"

B

C

A

D

D

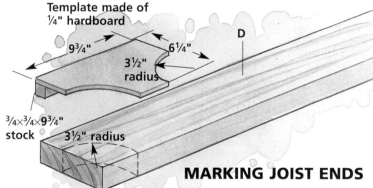

Template made of
$\frac{1}{4}$" hardboard

$9\frac{3}{4}$"

$6\frac{1}{4}$"

$3\frac{1}{2}$"
radius

D

$\frac{3}{4} \times \frac{3}{4} \times 9\frac{3}{4}$"
stock

$3\frac{1}{2}$" radius

MARKING JOIST ENDS

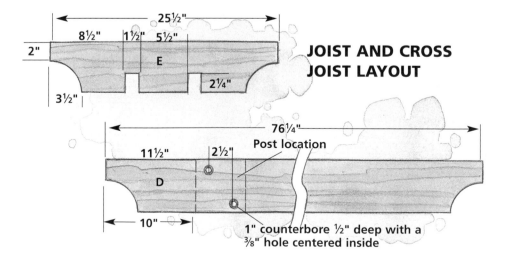

$25\frac{1}{2}$"

$8\frac{1}{2}$" $1\frac{1}{2}$" $5\frac{1}{2}$"

2"

E

$2\frac{1}{4}$"

$3\frac{1}{2}$"

**JOIST AND CROSS
JOIST LAYOUT**

$76\frac{1}{4}$"

Post location

$11\frac{1}{2}$" $2\frac{1}{2}$"

D

10"

1" counterbore $\frac{1}{2}$" deep with a
$\frac{3}{8}$" hole centered inside

Build a sturdy gate

1 Cut 14 1×6 boards 68 inches long for the slats (O). Chuck a $\frac{1}{8}$-inch round-over bit in your handheld router and rout the boards' outside ends and edges. Cut the two center slats for the window $15\frac{1}{2}$ inches from the top end, where shown on the Gate Exploded View drawing.

2 Clamp together several slats (O) edge to edge, facedown, positioning the long portion of one of the cut slats in the center. Make sure the bottom ends are flush and the assembly is square. Insert the short portion of the center slat, leaving a $5\frac{1}{2}$-inch-long space for the window. Measure the width of the assembly for the exact length of the 1×6 rails (P) and cut them to length. Cut the 1×6 stiles (Q) to 57 inches long.

3 Glue and clamp the bottom rail (P) in place. Drill countersunk shank holes, centered on the rail's width and on each slat where shown on the Gate Exploded View drawing. Drive in the screws. Glue, clamp, drill, and screw the stiles (Q) then the top rail (P) in place. When drilling the shank holes in the top rail, once again center each hole on a slat but drill them 1 inch from the rail's bottom edge.

4 Cut the brace (R) to 65 inches long. Lay it diagonally across the assembly with its top end at the hinge side. Mark and cut the end angles as shown in the Gate Exploded View drawing. Drill countersunk shank holes, and glue and screw the brace in place.

EXPLODED VIEW

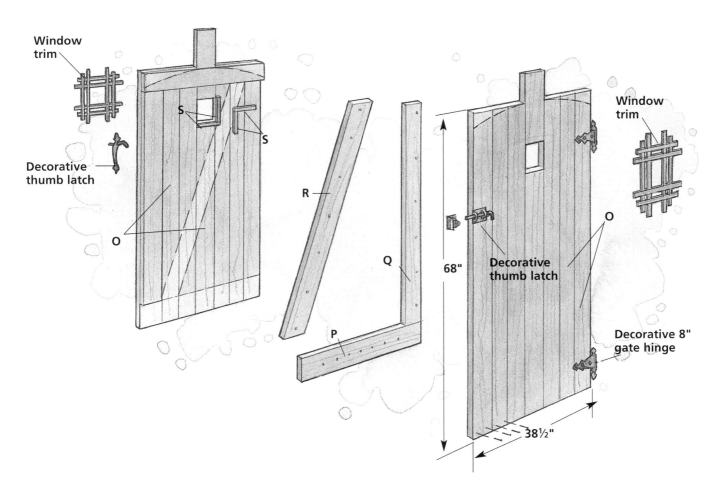

Window trim

Decorative thumb latch

S

S

O

R

Q

P

Window trim

68"

Decorative thumb latch

O

Decorative 8" gate hinge

38½"

5 Cut four ³/₄×³/₄×6¹/₄ window cleats (S) to size, apply glue, and nail them in place around the window with 3d galvanized box nails.

6 Apply glue to the rails, stiles, brace, and cleats. Clamp the remaining slats in place with the cut slat in the center. Using a thin wood strip bent to the curve shown in the Gate Exploded View drawing, mark the door's top arc. Drill countersunk screw holes in the slats and screw the slats to the rails, stiles, and brace. Remove the clamps. Cut the top arc with a jigsaw and sand it smooth. Rout ¹/₈-inch round-overs on both edges.

7 Cut the long and short window trim (T, U) to size. (See the illustration on page 91.) Install a ¹/₂-inch dado blade in your tablesaw and raise it to cut ³/₈ inch deep. Attach an auxiliary extension to your miter gauge and form the notches where shown. Apply glue to the joints and assemble the trim. With the glue dry, drill countersunk shank holes and screw the trim in place around the gate window.

8 Prime the gate with exterior acrylic latex primer, taking care to fully coat the end grain. Finish the gate with two coats of acrylic latex exterior paint.

Now put it all together

1 Clamp the main joists (D) to the posts where shown in the Final Assembly drawing *below*. Check the joists for level front to back and side to side. Using the screw holes in the joists as guides, drill pilot holes into the posts. Slip washers on the lag screws and drive them in.

FINAL ASSEMBLY

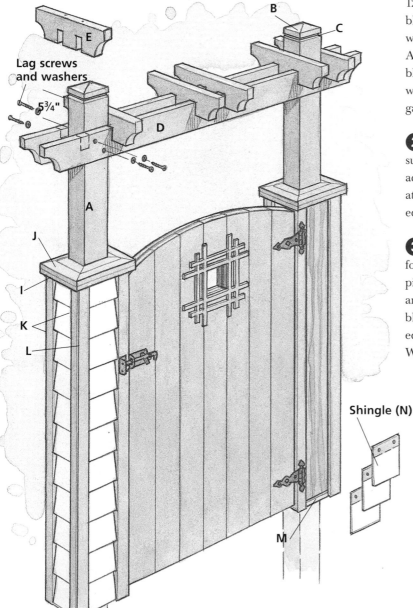

Lag screws and washers

5¾"

Shingle (N)

2 Place the cross joists (E) where shown on the Final Assembly drawing. The notches in the cross joists fit over the main joists. Drill countersunk shank holes through the cross joists at each notch. Drive 4-inch deck screws through the cross joists into the main joists.

Box and trim the posts

1 From 2×4 stock, cut 40 pieces 7 inches long for horizontal blocking (F) and two pieces 12⁵⁄₁₆ inches for hinge blocking (G). Fasten the blocking to the posts with 3-inch deck screws where shown in the Post Position and Surround Assembly drawing, page 87. Install the hinge blocking (G) on only the hinge-side post, flush with the corner that is in the direction of the gate's swing.

2 From exterior-grade plywood, cut the eight surround sides (H) to size. Using construction adhesive and 6d common galvanized nails, attach the sides to the blocking. Keep the top edges of the sides and the top blocking flush.

3 Cut eight ¾×1¾×14½-inch pieces of cedar for the trim bases (I), and eight 1½×4×14½-inch pieces of cedar for the beveled trim (J). Glue and clamp them together to make overlength blanks for the surround trim (I/J), keeping one edge of the assembly flush. Use an exterior glue. With the glue dry, cut the bevels.

4 Miter-cut the surround trim (I/J) to fit around the tops of the surrounds. Gluing the corners together, nail the surround trim to the blocking (F) with 10d galvanized finishing nails.

5 Cut eight ¾×1½-inch battens (K) and eight ¾×2¼-inch battens (L), each 66 inches long. Nail them to the corners of the post surrounds with 6d galvanized finishing nails where shown on the Post Position and Surround Assembly drawing.

WINDOW TRIM

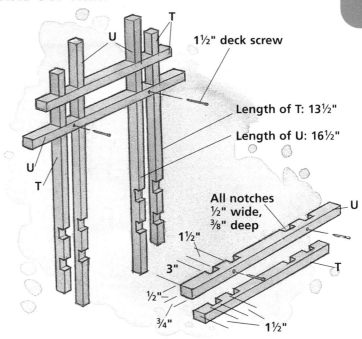

1½" deck screw

Length of T: 13½"

Length of U: 16½"

All notches ½" wide, ⅜" deep

1½"

3"

½"

¾"

1½"

Apply the shingles

1 Rip two ⁷⁄₁₆×¾×30-inch blanks for the starter strips (M). From these blanks, cut pieces to fit around the bottom of each post surround. Nail them in place with 4d galvanized box nails.

2 Using an inexpensive carbide-tipped blade in your tablesaw, trim 18-inch-long fiber-cement shingles (N) to width, then cut the lengths in half, making 8¹⁵⁄₁₆-inch-long shingles. You'll get two of these shingles out of each 18-inch one, so for the 88 shingles, you'll have to purchase at least 44 of the 18-inch shingles.

3 Fasten the shingles with a couple dabs of construction adhesive and 1¼-inch roofing nails, maintaining the 6-inch exposure as shown in the Final Assembly drawing. Keep the course lines even all around each post box. Because nothing overlaps the top course, trim these shingles to 6 inches before nailing them on.

4 Caulk the joint between the surround trim I/J and the post. Fill any nail holes. Prime and paint the shingles, battens, and trim. Touch up the paint on the posts and arbor where needed.

Hang the gate

1 Position the gate between the shingled post surrounds, flush with the corner battens, as shown in the Final Assembly drawing. Raise it 1½ inches off the ground with scrap-wood blocks and insert shims between the gate and the corner battens to make the gaps at both sides of the gate equal.

2 Position the hinges and mark the screw locations as shown at *right*. Drill pilot holes and fasten the hinges to the gate, then the post. Use the 1½-inch-long lag screws provided with the hinges to fasten the hinges to the gate, but use

4-inch-long lag screws for fastening into the post surround. Locate the T-ends of the hinges so that the pilot holes for the 4-inch lag screws go through the corner batten and into the hinge blocking (G).

3 Remove the shims and temporary supports. Install a latch according to the instructions that come with it.

Temporary support

Classic Arbor

Here's a structure that can provide a grand entrance to your yard or garden. You can start building the arbor in a garage or basement workshop during the winter, and assemble it outside when the weather warms. The project will keep you busy in your shop for a while, and the end result will make your grounds a showplace for years to come.

Set the posts

1 Stake posthole locations. To determine the locations of the wing posts (B) and main posts (A), cut the curved railings (D) first.

2 Using a router, chamfer the edges of four 10-foot-long posts (A). When laying out the chamfers, take into account the portion of the posts that will be set in concrete.

EXPLODED VIEW

Crossbeam Ends

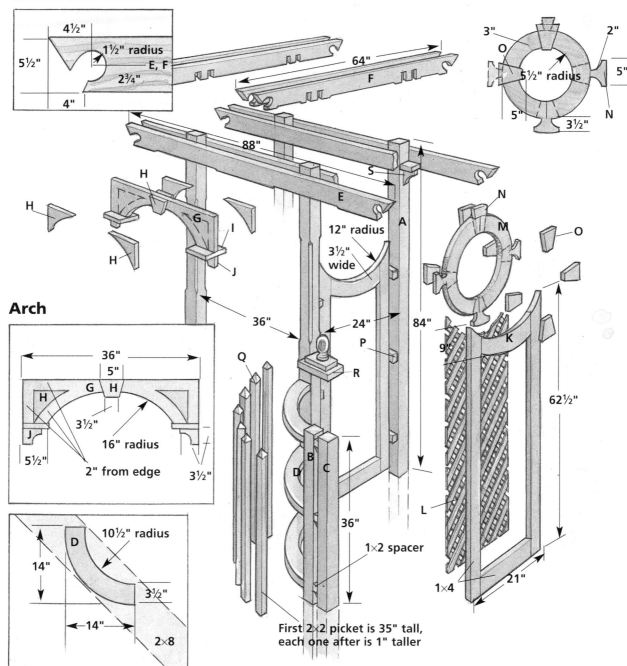

4½"
5½"
1½" radius
E, F
2¾"
4"

64"
F

3"
O
2"
5½" radius
5"
5"
N
3½"

88"
S
E
A
N
M
O

H
H
G
I
H
J

12" radius
3½" wide
84"

Arch

36"
5"
G H
H
3½"
16" radius
2" from edge
5½"
3½"
J

36"
24"
P
R
Q
B
C
D
36"
9"
K
L
62½"
1×4
21"

10½" radius
14"
D
3½"
14"
2×8

1×2 spacer

First 2×2 picket is 35" tall,
each one after is 1" taller

3 Use 6-foot 4×4s for wing posts (B and C). Nail 1×2 spacer blocks on B; clamp C in place with bar clamps.

4 Set the posts in concrete as shown on page 164. Check them for plumb and hold the posts in place with temporary 2×4 bracing.

5 After the concrete cures, cut each 4×4 post to its finished height. First cut one main post to height, then use a level on a length of 2×4 to establish the height of the other main posts (A). Repeat this process for the wing posts.

6 Toenail the curved railings (D) in place with 8d casing nails.

Top it off

1 Cut four 2×6 crossbeams (E). Lay out end cuts with a compass and protractor. Using a jigsaw, cut the designs; chamfer bottom edges of each board. Attach the crossbeams (E) to main posts (A) with 16d common nails.

2 Cut four 2×6 rafters (F). Make end cuts identical to the crossbeams (E). Using a jigsaw, cut notches in the bottoms of the rafters (F) to fit snugly over the crossbeams (E). Chamfer the bottom edges. Nail the rafters to the posts (A).

3 Using a jigsaw, cut two sides (G) from 1×10s. Cut trim pieces (H) from ¾-inch stock. Rout edges; attach the trim to the sides.

4 Cut pieces (I) from 1×6s and (J) from 2×4 blocking. Attach to the sides.

Add the lattice

1 To make the lattice frames (K), cut the bottoms and sides from 1×4s; use 1×10s for the curved top pieces. Cut the curved pieces with a jigsaw. Dowel the frames together using ⅜×2-inch dowel pins and exterior glue.

2 Cut 2 pieces of 21×63-inch lattice (L) from a 4×8-foot sheet of ¼-inch diagonal lattice or make your own lattice as shown on pages 160–161. Lay the lattice frame (K) over the sheet and cut the lattice 1 inch smaller than the outside of the frame.

3 Attach 2×2 blocks (P) to the posts (A); toenail one lattice frame to the blocks. Hold the lattice in place; secure the other frame piece over it. Use deck screws so that the lattice can be easily replaced if damaged. The lattice should fit loosely between the frames to allow for swelling during humid conditions.

4 Lay out the circle designs (M) on exterior ½-inch plywood. Using a jigsaw, cut two half circles with an inside radius of 5½ inches and an outside radius of 8½ inches.

5 Using ⅜×2-inch dowel pins, dowel the half circles (M) together and dowel ½-inch plywood trim pieces (N) into circles (M). Cut parts O and nail them to N with 4d finishing nails.

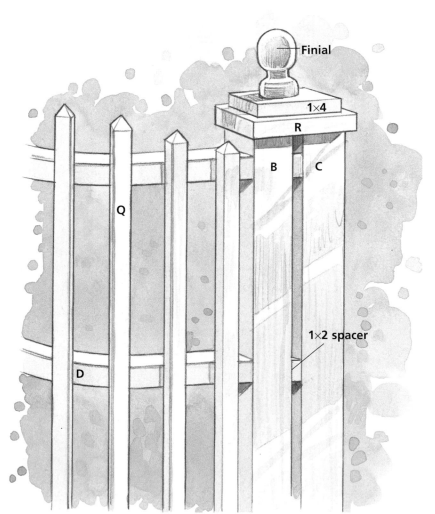

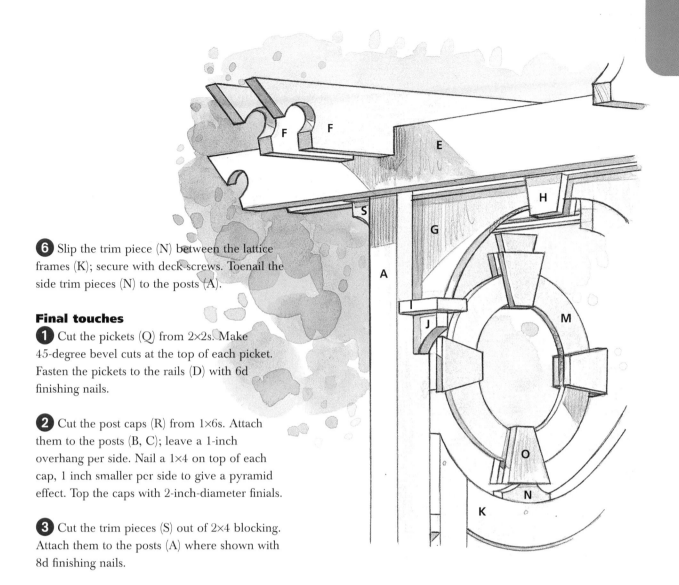

6 Slip the trim piece (N) between the lattice frames (K); secure with deck screws. Toenail the side trim pieces (N) to the posts (A).

Final touches

1 Cut the pickets (Q) from 2×2s. Make 45-degree bevel cuts at the top of each picket. Fasten the pickets to the rails (D) with 6d finishing nails.

2 Cut the post caps (R) from 1×6s. Attach them to the posts (B, C); leave a 1-inch overhang per side. Nail a 1×4 on top of each cap, 1 inch smaller per side to give a pyramid effect. Top the caps with 2-inch-diameter finials.

3 Cut the trim pieces (S) out of 2×4 blocking. Attach them to the posts (A) where shown with 8d finishing nails.

FENCE FACTS

Fences and arbors just naturally go together, but be sure you have a plan before you set a post in the ground. First find out if there are underground utilities where you intend to dig. Contact your local utilities to have a locator mark routes of underground gas, telephone, and electrical lines.

■ For fences that follow a property line, find out about any setback and height requirements. Your local building code official can help you with this. If you know the location of your lot corner stakes, lay out your fence along a string stretched between them. If you are unsure where your lot corners are,

hire a surveyor to mark them. This is likely to be expensive, but may prevent problems later.

■ With the position of your fence line determined, mark the post locations with stakes driven into the ground along the string. Start by deciding approximately how long each fence panel should measure, then divide the total fence run by this length. Your fence will probably not neatly divide into an even number of these increments, so adjust the posts' center-to-center distances to make all the fence panels the same size.

KNOCK-DOWN ARBOR

Set this elegant structure up in the spring and the piece will occupy center stage in your landscaping all summer long. Then, at the first frost of fall, you can dismantle it into three sections that store flat.

Cut and assemble the frame

1 From 2×4 stock, cut four uprights (A) 81½ inches, two beams (B) 63½ inches, and two crossbeams (C) 39¼ inches.

2 Mount a ⅜-inch dado set on your tablesaw and cut a full-length, ⅜-inch-deep groove along the center of the inside face of each upright. Cut a 6½-inch-long half lap ¾ inch deep in the top end of the outside face of each upright for the half-lap joints, shown on the Post Half Lap illustration on page 99. Now lay out and cut a 3½-inch-wide mating half lap starting 7¾ inches in from each end of both beams, shown on the Top Frame drawing on page 98.

CUTTING NOTCH

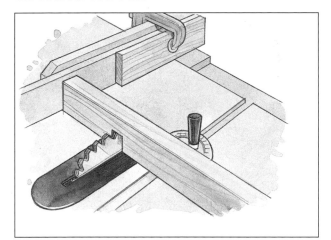

▲ The rip fence acts as a stop for the inside end of the edge-lap notch and a ¾"-thick board clamped to the fence serves as a stop for the outside end.

SQUARING TOP

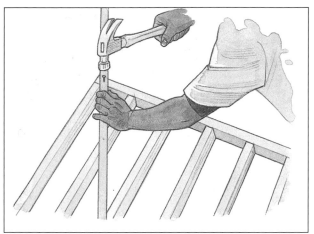

▲ Square the top grid assembly by measuring diagonally in both directions. When these dimensions are equal, tack on a diagonal strip to keep the assembly square.

3 Lay out 1½-inch-wide notches 1¾ inches deep on the beams for the four edge-lap joints. To do this, mark a notch starting 4¾ inches from each end on the bottom edge of the crossbeams. Elevate the blade to 1¾ inches and use a miter gauge to cut all eight notches.

4 Make enlarged copies of the end pattern shown on page 99. Adhere one pattern to each end of both beams. Before sawing, refer to the Top Frame drawing on page 98 for the correct orientation of the patterns on the beams and crossbeams. Similarly cut the crossbeams.

Assemble the top grid

1 For the top grid, rip and crosscut six pieces ¾×1½×49¼ inches (D) and six pieces ¾×1½×26¾ inches (E). Next, assemble the top grid as shown in the drawing, *right.* After attaching a crosspiece (E) to each end of the six long members (D), square the assembly by measuring diagonally and tack on a diagonal strip to hold the assembly square as shown in the illustration, *top right.*

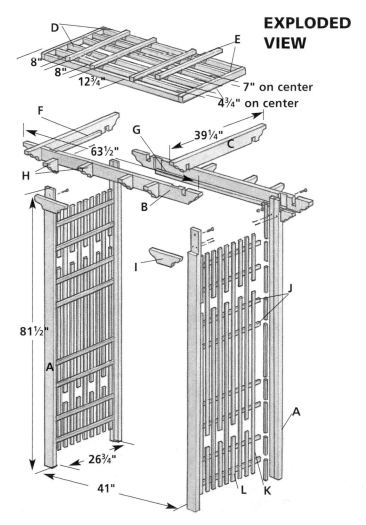

EXPLODED VIEW

8"
8"
12¾"
7" on center
4¾" on center
39¼"
63½"
81½"
26¾"
41"

TOP FRAME

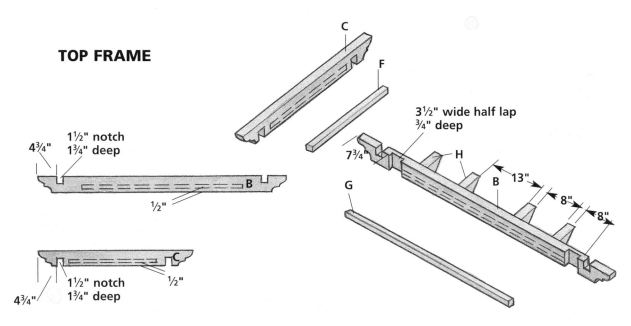

4³/₄" 1½" notch 1¾" deep ½" B

1½" notch 1¾" deep ½" C 4³/₄"

C F 3½" wide half lap ¾" deep 7¾" H 13" B 8" 8" G

2 Cut two support cleats ³/₄×³/₄×22³/₄ inches (F) and two ³/₄×³/₄×40 inches (G). Glue and screw them to the beams and crossbeams ½ inch above the bottom edge where shown *above*.

3 Place the top grid assembly inside the beam/crossbeam assembly so that the top grid rests on the cleats. Using a combination square, transfer the location of each part E onto the face and edge of each beam (B) so that you can align each corbel (H) with a corresponding E.

4 To make the corbels (H), stack and clamp two 24-inch lengths of leftover 2×4 and adhere four copies of the end pattern (*opposite page*) to the top face. Bandsaw the contoured ends to shape, then crosscut the corbels to length. Glue and screw four corbels (H) to each beam, one at each crosspiece (E) location.

5 Make four enlarged copies of the half pattern for the decorative trim (I) shown on the *opposite page*. Tape two pairs together along the centerlines to make two full patterns. Cut four pieces of ³/₄-inch-thick stock to 3×11 inches. Stack two pairs of pieces using double-face tape, attach the two full patterns, and bandsaw the parts to shape.

Now for the lattice

1 Rip 22 strips ³/₈×96 inches from ³/₄-inch stock. Set up a table-mounted router and rout ³/₁₆-inch round-overs on all edges of 18 strips. For your latticework, cut 16 crosspieces (J) 27½ inches long, 18 long verticals (K) 53 inches long, and 18 short verticals (L) 13 inches long. Cut spacers M through Q, shown in the Side Panel drawing *opposite*, from four strips.

2 Lay out the position of each crosspiece (J) on the edge of one upright (A) where shown on the Side Panel drawing *opposite*. Place this upright at the edge of your workbench and clamp it there. Next, clamp a piece of scrap wood square to the upright 2³/₄ inches from the bottom of the bottom crosspiece. Now align the 18 long verticals in this squared corner. Use your framing square to transfer each set of crosspiece lines onto the strips as shown in the Crosspiece Layout illustration *opposite*.

3 Lay out your lattice panels using the Side Panel drawing as a guide. First clamp a second 2×4 at the other end of the upright to square the top end of the lattice. From ³/₈-inch scrap, cut 10 spacers 2³/₈ inches long and about 100 that

POST HALF LAP

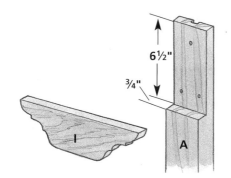

6½"

¾"

I

A

CROSSPIECE LAYOUT

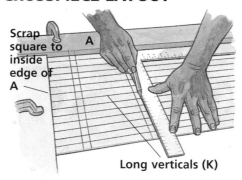

Scrap square to inside edge of A

A

Long verticals (K)

LAYING OUT LATTICEWORK

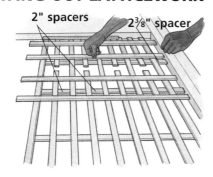

2" spacers

2⅜" spacer

END PATTERN

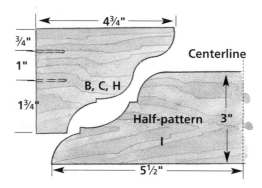

4¾"

¾"

1"

1¾"

B, C, H

Centerline

Half-pattern

3"

I

5½"

◄ Brass carriage bolts on top hold the assembly together. For footings, drill holes in strips of steel, partially sink them into concrete, and bolt the arbor uprights (A) to the steel.

SIDE PANEL

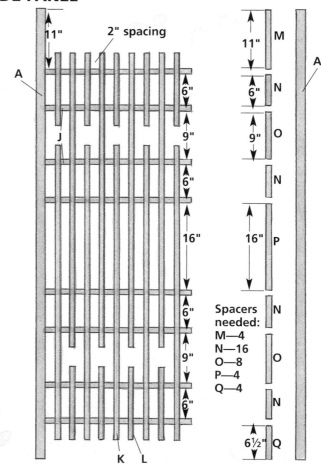

11"

2" spacing

A

J

6"

9"

6"

16"

6"

9"

6"

K   L

M

11"

N

6"

O

9"

N

16"   P

Spacers needed:
M—4
N—16
O—8
P—4
Q—4

N

O

N

6½"   Q

A

are 2 inches long. Use the longer spacers between the uprights and the outside lattice strips and the shorter spacers between pairs of vertical strips as shown in the Laying Out Latticework illustration *above*.

4 Lay out the outer verticals first, using the longer spacers. Then add the short verticals and lay the crosspieces over the top. Working one crosspiece at a time, apply a dab of glue at each junction, then nail the crosspiece in place with #18×⅝-inch brass escutcheon pins.

Bolt the arbor together

1 Transfer the crosspiece positions to the grooved faces of the remaining uprights. Next, glue and screw a decorative trim piece (I) to the bottom of the half lap on each upright. Glue and clamp the crossbeams (C) to the beams (B) and the top grid to the support cleats.

2 Fit an upright into each half lap so that the frame will stand by itself. At each corner, drill a ⅜-inch hole through the beam, the upright, and the long grid member. Attach the parts together with a ⅜×3-inch brass carriage bolt, a flat washer, a split washer, and a nut.

SPLIT-LEVEL ARBOR

Sturdy and stylish, this two-level arbor offers places for plants to grow and shady seating. It consists of 4×4 framing topped with 2×4 rafters and sided with lattice. Uncomplicated construction makes it possible to build this attractive arbor in a couple of weekends, including the time it takes to dig eight postholes below the frost line.

Set the posts first

1 Start by setting the four tallest posts, located 48 inches apart. Set them in concrete as explained on page 164. Before adding the concrete, make sure each post is plumb in all directions. Add rocks to the bottom of the postholes to bring the tops of the posts level with one another.

EXPLODED VIEW

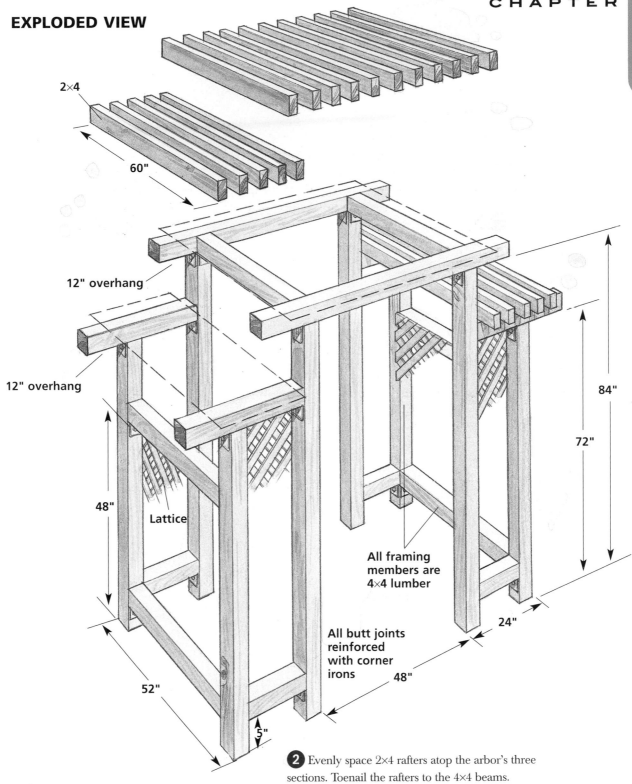

2×4

60"

12" overhang

12" overhang

48"

Lattice

84"

72"

All framing
members are
4×4 lumber

All butt joints
reinforced
with corner
irons

24"

48"

52"

5"

2 Next, set the shorter posts and check them for plumb. Locate them 2 feet away from the longer posts, as shown in the illustration *above*.

Install the horizontal framing and rafters

1 Secure 4×4 crosspieces to the post structure with corner angle irons and 2-inch screws.

2 Evenly space 2×4 rafters atop the arbor's three sections. Toenail the rafters to the 4×4 beams.

Add the lattice

1 Buy prefabricated lattice panels and cut them to fit or build your own latticework as shown on page 160.

2 Nail the lattice panels to the inside surfaces of the framework.

BASIC PERGOLA

with nothing solid to lean an extension ladder on. You'll need help to raise some of the members into place. Line up helpers in advance and host a pergola-building party.

Start with the corners

The pergola is constructed by first cutting and positioning the 4×4 corner posts, then setting the overhead framing in place.

1 Begin by trimming the corner posts to 10 feet. Soak the bottom 18 inches of each post in wood preservative.

2 Set the posts in position and temporarily brace them. On paved areas, anchor the braces with concrete blocks as shown in the Setting Posts illustration, *opposite*. Otherwise, stake them in place. Check that each is plumb.

If you want to bring some shade to an unsheltered patio, consider building a trellis-like pergola. You can assemble this airy, yet sturdy, structure in two or three weekends. Ideal for climbing plants, it creates an area of dappled sunlight that's delightful for entertaining. You can make it as shady as you like by adding climbing plants and creepers, or by topping the pergola with awning canvas. The four corners of the pergola are anchored with planter boxes.

Getting ready

This project calls for no special tools, but a hammer drill for boring into concrete and a power mitersaw will make the job easier. Also, have two 12-foot stepladders on hand. While you are building the structure will be unsteady,

Build the top frame and add more posts

1 With the help of a friend or two, construct the top frame in place with 2×6s and 3-inch galvanized screws. Fasten the frame to the corner posts with angled 3-inch deck screws or three-sided corner brackets. Space inside joists 80 inches apart, center to center.

2 To mark positions on the patio for the intermediate posts, drop a plumb bob from each of the points where lateral joists connect with the perimeter beams. With a masonry bit and heavy-duty drill, bore holes in the concrete for the shields and securely attach U-brackets with lag-screw shields and screws (see page 104).

EXPLODED VIEW

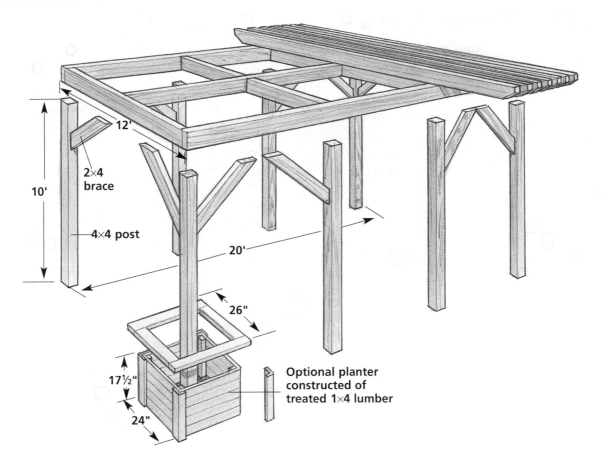

12'

2×4 brace

10'

4×4 post

20'

26"

17½"

24"

Optional planter constructed of treated 1×4 lumber

SETTING POSTS

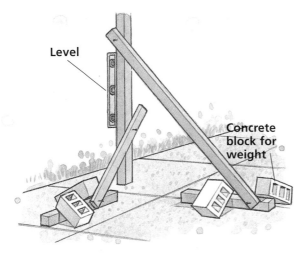

Level

Concrete block for weight

▲ Plumb the four corner posts and brace them in place as shown. Using single screws to attach the braces makes it easier to adjust them and to remove them later.

TOP FRAME

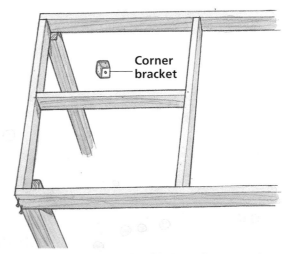

Corner bracket

▲ Connect the corner posts with 2×6s, then screw lateral joists in place where the intermediate posts will be located. Corner brackets make it easier to attach the 2×6s to the posts.

BASIC PERGOLA (CONTINUED)

INTERMEDIATE POSTS

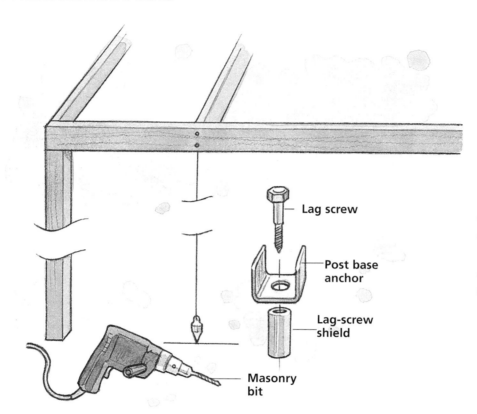

Lag screw

Post base anchor

Lag-screw shield

Masonry bit

◀ Drop a plumb bob on a chalk line to locate points where intermediate posts will attach to the patio. Drill holes in the paving and set post anchors with shields and lag screws.

ATTACHING INTERMEDIATE POSTS

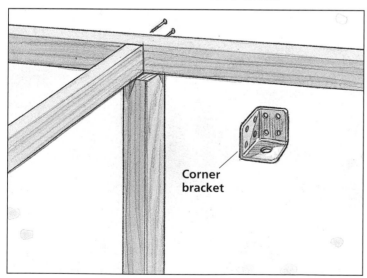

Corner bracket

▲ Attach the intermediate posts to the top frame with screws or screws and corner brackets. Screw the U-brackets to the bottoms of the posts.

3 Trim each of the remaining posts to size, taking into account how high the anchors will hold them off the slab. The posts also may differ in length due to variations in the slab. Drill a hole in the bottom of each post to fit over the lag screw head. Set each post into its bracket place, check for plumb, and attach the post to the frame with angle-driven screws or corner brackets.

Install braces and rafters
1 On the overhead 2×6s, mark the halfway point between each pair of posts. Measure and mark the same distance down from the top of each post. Measure between these marks and the centerpoint mark to determine the length of the long side of each 2×4 angled brace. Cut

DIAGONAL BRACES

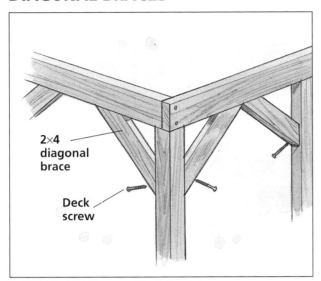

▲ Strengthen the structure with diagonal braces at each post. Determine and mark the midpoints between posts, then measure the same dimension down the posts. Measure from post to midpoint and cut braces with 45-degree angles at each end. Screw the braces to the posts as shown.

both ends of each brace at a 45-degree angle. Attach them to the overhead and posts with 3-inch deck screws.

2 Cut angled ends on 16-foot 2×6 rafters as shown in teh Installing Rafters illustration. After you've cut a number of rafters, experiment with different rafter spacings: Closer together, they create more shade. Attach the rafters with hurricane ties and 1-inch screws.

Build the planter boxes
1 Construct the four corner planter boxes around the posts, attaching 1×4s to 2×2 framing with 1⅝-inch screws. Butt the corners together, line with 4-mil plastic sheeting held in place with staples, and cover the boxes' outside corners with 1×4 trim pieces.

2 Top off each planter with a 1×4 ledge and fill the box with soil. The soil's weight will anchor the corner posts in place.

INSTALLING RAFTERS

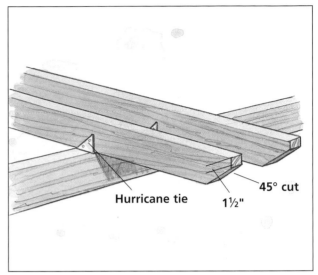

▲ To cut the rafter ends, measure 1½ inches from the top of each rafter and make a 45-degree-angle cut. Fasten the rafters to the top frame with screws and hurricane ties. The number and spacing of rafters you decide on depends on the amount of shade you want.

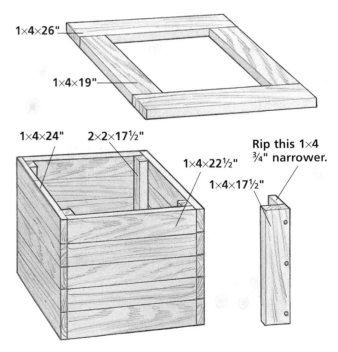

▲ Construct boxes for the four corner planters with 1×4s and 2×2s as shown. Filled with soil (and your favorite plantings), they will anchor the posts and add beauty to your patio.

RELAXATION STATION

Put your patio in the swing of things with this gracious pergola. If you don't have an existing surface to bolt it to, you can pour concrete footings.

Put posts and rails together

1 Cut the 4×4 posts (A) to 91¼ inches. Cut eight 2×4 rails 12 inches long (B) and four 2×4 rails 48 inches long (C).

2 Mark the locations of the side rails (B) and the end rails (C) on the posts. (See the Arbor End drawing on page 108.)

3 Drill two pocket holes in the underside of each rail (B, C). Set the pocket-hole jig back 1 inch from the end as shown in the Drilling Pocket Holes illustration on page 108.

4 Assemble two posts (A) and two side rails (B) with screws as shown in the Arbor End drawing. To make assembly easier, brace the rail against a handscrew clamped to the post and clamp it in position.

5 Rip ³⁄₈-inch strips for the lattice (D, E, F) from 2×4 stock. Cut to the lengths shown on page 109, *bottom right*.

6 Rip more 2×4 stock to ³⁄₈ inch for the lattice stops (G–L). Rip and crosscut the resulting ³⁄₈×1½-inch stock to the dimensions shown for the stops in the Arbor End drawing.

7 Rip and crosscut enough ³⁄₈×½-inch stock for the spacers shown on the Arbor End drawing. You'll need 112 of the 3¹⁵⁄₁₆-inch spacers, 32 of the 4³⁄₁₆-inch ones, and 16 of the 5¼-inch pieces.

EXPLODED VIEW

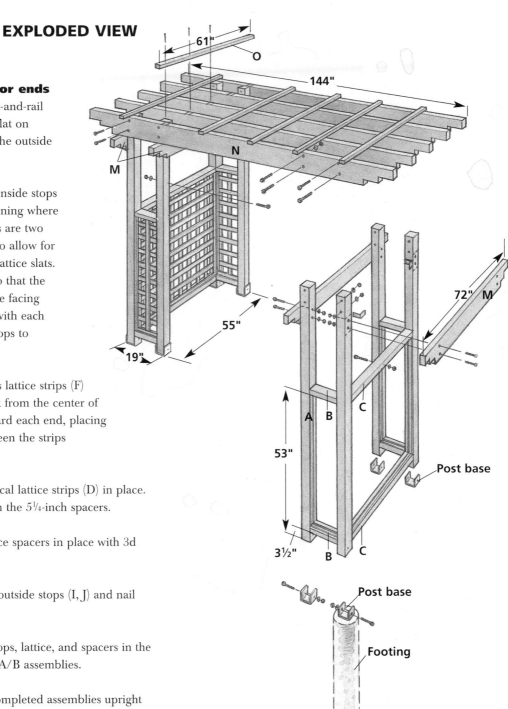

Build the arbor ends

1 Lay one post-and-rail assembly (A, B) flat on sawhorses, with the outside facing up.

2 Position the inside stops (G, H) in the opening where shown. The stops are two different widths to allow for the overlapping lattice slats. Place the stops so that the outer edges (those facing down) are flush with each other. Nail the stops to the posts.

3 Lay the cross lattice strips (F) in position. Work from the center of the opening toward each end, placing the spacers between the strips as shown.

4 Lay the vertical lattice strips (D) in place. Center them with the 5¼-inch spacers.

5 Nail the lattice spacers in place with 3d finishing nails.

6 Position the outside stops (I, J) and nail them in place.

7 Install the stops, lattice, and spacers in the remaining three A/B assemblies.

8 Stand two completed assemblies upright and parallel to each other, inside facing inside. Position the end rails (C) between the corner posts, and fasten them with pocket-hole screws.

9 Install the inner stops (G, K), the lattice strips (D, E), the spacers, and the outer stops (I, L) as you did in the side panels.

10 Where the lattice strips cross, nail them together with #16×¾-inch escutcheon pins.

Raise the roof

1 If not already done, install the post bases on the footings.

2 Stand the assembled end sections in the post bases, with their open sides facing.

DRILLING POCKET HOLES

▲ Scrap wood 1" wide (shown in yellow) serves as a spacer when drilling the tails with the pocket-hole jig. Setting the jig 1" from the end centers the screw on the rail, allowing longer screws.

ATTACHING RAILS

B

A

▲ A handscrew clamp and a bar clamp hold the rail (B) in position when attaching it to the post (A) with deck screws. Construct three more A/B assemblies in this way.

ARBOR END

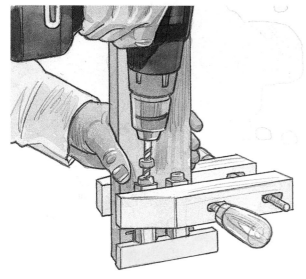

$3^{15}/_{16}$" spacer

$4^{3}/_{16}$" spacer

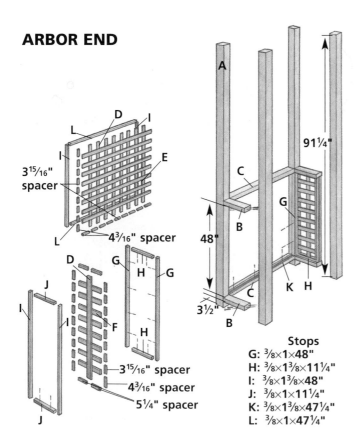

$3^{15}/_{16}$" spacer

$4^{3}/_{16}$" spacer

$5^{1}/_{4}$" spacer

A

91¼"

C

B

G

48"

3½"

B

C

K   H

B

Stops
G: ³/₈×1×48"
H: ³/₈×1³/₈×11¼"
I: ³/₈×1³/₈×48"
J: ³/₈×1×11¼"
K: ³/₈×1³/₈×47¼"
L: ³/₈×1×47¼"

Ensure that the units are plumb and level, then secure them to the bases.

3 Cut the crossbeams (M) and rafters (N) to the lengths shown. Cut the ends to the shape shown on the Exploded View drawing.

4 Drill ½-inch bolt holes where shown in the four crossbeams and two of the rafters. The rafters with holes drilled in them will go on the outside of each arbor end, as shown in the Exploded View drawing.

5 Position the crossbeams (M) where shown on the posts (A). Make sure they're level and aligned across the tops; then clamp them in place. Drill ½-inch holes through the posts, guiding through the holes in the crossbeams.

6 Position the two outer rafters (N) where shown. Drill bolt holes and bolt the rafters to the posts.

ATTACHING RAILS

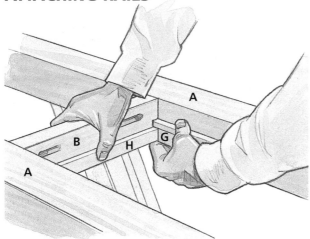

▲ The inner faces of the stops are offset by ⅜" to accommodate the overlapping lattice strips. Place the stops so that their outer edges (those facing down) are flush with each other.

7 Space the remaining three rafters evenly across the top of the crossbeams as shown. Toenail them to the crossbeams or attach them with screws in pocket holes, drilled from the back side.

SECTION VIEW

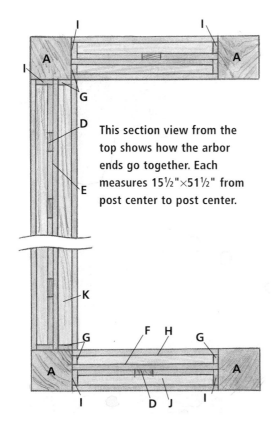

This section view from the top shows how the arbor ends go together. Each measures 15½"×51½" from post center to post center.

LATTICE STRIPS

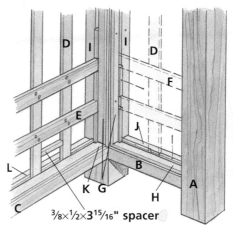

⅜×½×3¹⁵⁄₁₆" spacer

▲ Lattice strips, separated by spacers, fit between stops nailed to the posts and rails. Fasten the components with 3d nails or speed the job along with a pneumatic brad nailer.

8 Cut six 1×2 top cleats (O) to 61 inches long. Position them across the tops of the rafters where shown. Screw the cleats to the rafters.

9 Place some lawn furniture in the pergola, or you can build or buy a porch swing to hang in it, as shown in the opening illustration.

▼ Space lattice for the side panels and end panels as shown here. If you plan to stain or prime and paint the lattice for your pergola, save time by sanding and applying the finish before installing the strips. Fasten strips together by driving escutcheon pins from the inside while holding the head of another hammer or heavy piece of metal against the joint on the outside.

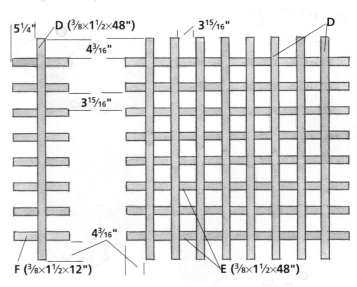

5¼" D (⅜×1½×48")   3¹⁵⁄₁₆"   D

4³⁄₁₆"

3¹⁵⁄₁₆"

4³⁄₁₆"

F (⅜×1½×12")   E (⅜×1½×48")

BUILD-TO-SUIT PERGOLA

Construct this project as a freestanding structure on an existing deck or patio, as shown *opposite*, or set its posts in the ground, *below*. No matter which way you go, you'll appreciate how quickly and easily this pergola goes together. You start with a pile of machined parts, raise the posts, construct the frames, then fit the slotted canopy subassemblies together.

Cut the parts

1 Cut four 6×6 (5½×5½ inches actual size) posts (A) 107¾ inches long. Sand the posts with progressively finer sandpaper, ending with 120-grit, and set them aside.

2 For the post caps, start by cutting four 1½×5½×5½-inch cap tops (B) and four ¾×4½×4½-inch cap bases (C). Bevel the 1½-inch cap tops where shown, *opposite, below left.* Sand the caps and set them aside. (You can install the caps after you have completely assembled the pergola.)

3 Cut the 2×6 main joists (D) and side girders (E) to 168 inches long. Make the marking/trimming template shown on page 112 and use it to mark 3½-inch-radius cutouts on the ends.

4 Turn the joists and girders upside down on a pair of sawhorses and clamp them together with their ends and edges flush. Using a square, draw lines across the bottom edges for 1½-inch-wide notches. Cut the notches as shown on page 112.

5 Take two of the parts just notched and clamp them together, with ends and edges flush. Use a handsaw and chisel to deepen the notches to $2^3/4$ inches (or half the actual width of your 2×6s). Mark these as the side girders (E) that, along with the end girders (H), form the pergola's frame.

6 Cut the 2×6 blocking (F) to 22 inches long and the 2×6 upper bracket cleats (G) to $8^3/8$ inches long.

7 Cut the 2×6 end girders (H) to 131 inches long and the stub joists (I) to $15^1/2$ inches long. Use the template, jigsaw, and router to mark and form the end cutouts.

8 Following the same procedure as with the main joists and side girders, form notches in the end girders (H) and the stub joists (I).

9 Cut eight 2×8 blanks $41^7/8$ inches long for the brackets (J). Cut the angled ends and curves where shown on the drawing on page 114.

10 Cut the lower bracket cleats (K) to size. Rout the $1/4$-inch cove and drill three shank holes countersunk from the back and six countersunk from the front in each piece where shown on page 114.

11 For the cove caps (L) and base trim (M), plane two 1×6×72-inch cedar boards to $3/4$ inch thick.(Cedar boards sold by some lumberyards are thicker.) Joint one edge of each board. Rout a $1/2$-inch cove in the jointed edges and rip off a $3/4$-inch strip for the cove caps (L). Joint the sawn edges of the remaining boards and rip them to $3^1/4$ inches wide for the base trim (M). Miter-cut the cove caps and base trim for the posts after the pergola is in place.

CUT THE POSTS

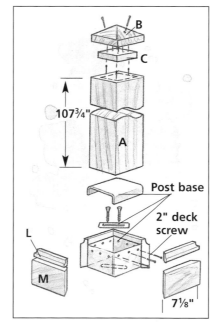

The posts are anchored by metal post bases and topped with pyramid-shaped caps. Mitered trim conceals the bases.

CUT ENDS

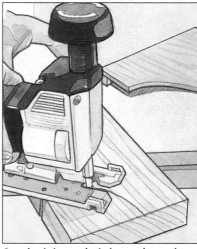

Cut the joist and girder ends to shape with a jigsaw, then complete the final profile with a router. Mark these cuts with the template shown in the background here. For a closer look at the template, see the drawing on *page 112, top left.*

BUILD-TO-SUIT PERGOLA (CONTINUED)

END TEMPLATE

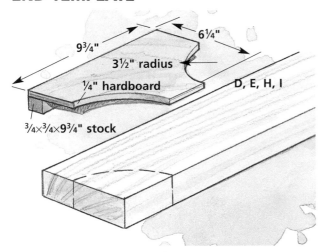

Make a template for marking the main joists (D), side girders (E), end girders (H), and stub joists (I). Cut two 3½-inch radii in ¼-inch hardboard. Nail the hardboard to ¾-inch-square stock so that you can easily and accurately position the template. Cut close with a jigsaw or bandsaw, then rout to the lines with a pattern bit and the template, working from the cutout's heel to the end of the board. Round-over the curves' edges.

SAWING NOTCHES

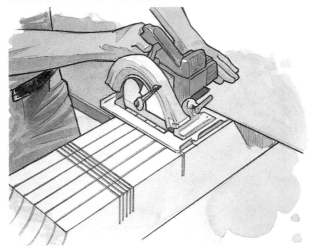

Use a portable circular saw, a framing square, and a 1-inch chisel to cut notches in the joists and girders. Mark the 1½-inch-wide notches with the square. Set the saw blade to cut 2¼ inches deep. Clamp the square to the joists and girders to serve as a guide for the saw, then cut a series of closely spaced kerfs to define the notches. (Although the illustration shows two stages of the operation on the same lumber, none of the parts for the pergola have two such closely spaced notches.)

CLEANING NOTCHES

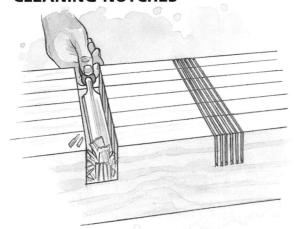

Use a chisel and hammer to clean out the notches to a uniform depth. Check the fit of your 1½-inch stock in the notches. For a good appearance and easy assembly, you'll want a close but not tight fit. You can also cut the notches on a tablesaw or radial-arm saw or by making a series of passes with a router. (Although the illustration shows two stages of the operation on the same lumber, none of the parts for the pergola have two such closely spaced notches.)

JOIST BLOCKING

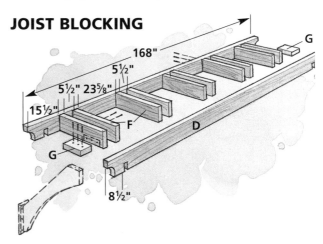

Prime all the pergola parts with an exterior-grade latex primer, applying two coats to the more absorbent end grain and notches. When the primer dries, lightly sand with 220-grit sandpaper. Finish all of the parts with two coats of exterior-grade latex paint. The pergola is then ready for final assembly as shown *opposite* and on the pages that follow.

ASSEMBLING JOISTS

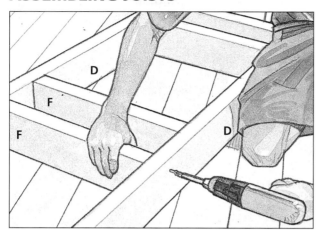

2×6×22-inch blocking (F) ties the main joists together. Drill countersunk holes through the joists and secure the blocking with 3-inch deck screws. Screw together the main joist/blocking (D/F) subassemblies where shown in the drawing *opposite, lower right*. Fasten the upper bracket cleats (G) to the assemblies where shown on the illustration *below right*. The brackets will attach to the cleats and posts during final assembly. For more about the brackets, see page 114, *upper left*.

POST BASE

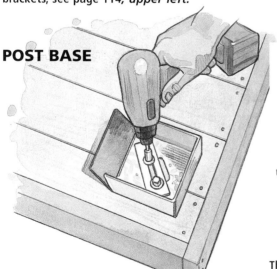

Lay out your pergola's footprint, and lag-screw four post bases to the deck. Take diagonal measurements to check your layout for square. (If the measurements are equal, the layout is square.) If the layout is not perfectly square, slots in the post bases provide wiggle room that allows you to fine-tune their locations. Don't worry about the bases' appearance. You'll cover them up with mitered trim, as shown on *page 115*.

ATTACHING BLOCKING

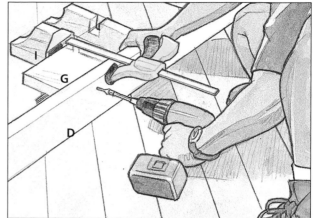

Screw together the two main joist/stub joist (D/I) subassemblies where shown *below*. Each subassembly consists of three main joists, 10 blocking pieces, and 10 stub joists. Your pergola's canopy is now complete and ready to top off the structure. All that remains is to erect the posts, tie them together with girders, and install the canopy. One beauty of this project is that you can get a jump on spring by precutting and finishing all the components in your shop, then assembling them outside on the first nice day.

STUB JOISTS

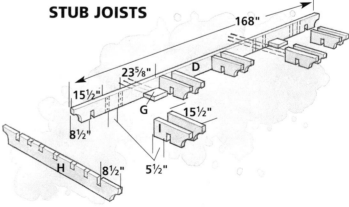

The main joist and end girder assemblies will look like this. The pergola shown is 148 inches long by 111 inches wide, outside of post to outside of post. You can adapt these dimensions to suit your site. But because 16 feet is the longest commonly available cedar 2×6 and the girders and joists extend beyond the footprint by 10 inches at each end, your footprint cannot exceed 172×172 inches. For any size, keep the distance between the closely spaced girders at 5½ inches. The posts shown are 107¾ inches tall. If you sink your posts into the ground, you'll need additional length to get below the frost line in your region.

BRACKET

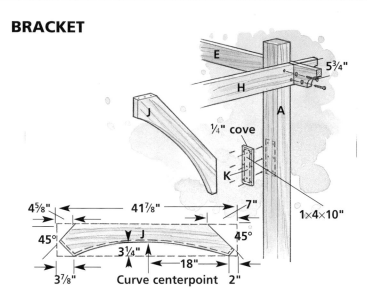

To draw the bracket curves, mark the centerpoint on one 2×8 blank. Bend a narrow strip of hardboard to join the centerpoint and ends, draw a curve, and cut it with a jigsaw. Use this as a template to draw curves on the other blanks.

Put it all together

1 Now that you have all your pergola parts made, primed, and painted, you're just an afternoon away from transforming your yard's personality. Referring to the sequence of drawings that starts on page 113 and ends on the *opposite page*, make up the subassemblies, erect the posts and girders, and install the canopy and braces. All you'll need is some basic hardware: deck screws, lag screws, and steel post bases. To securely anchor the post bases, add blocking underneath the deck. When lag-screwing the girders to the posts, drill counterbored shank holes through the girders and $\frac{1}{4}$-inch pilot holes into the posts. When fastening parts with deck screws, drill only countersunk shank holes. The deck screws drive into the cedar without needing pilot holes.

2 Finish off your pergola by driving 3-inch deck screws through the side girders (E) and the end girders (H) into the upper bracket cleats (G). Remove the temporary braces from the posts. Drill countersunk shank holes through the post caps (B/C). Apply construction adhesive to

ERECTING END GIRDER

Lag-screw each end girder (H) to two posts. Stand these assemblies up in the post bases, plumb, and brace them in place. Screw the bases to the posts.

GIRDER ASSEMBLY

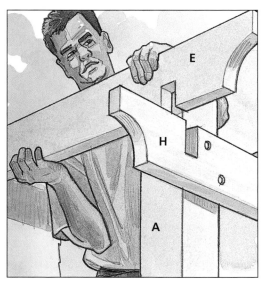

Slip the end notches of the side girders (E) into the notches of the end girders (H). Drill $\frac{1}{4}$-inch pilot holes and lag-screw the side girders to the posts.

the bottoms of the caps and screw the caps to the tops of the posts. Touch up the paint or finish where needed.

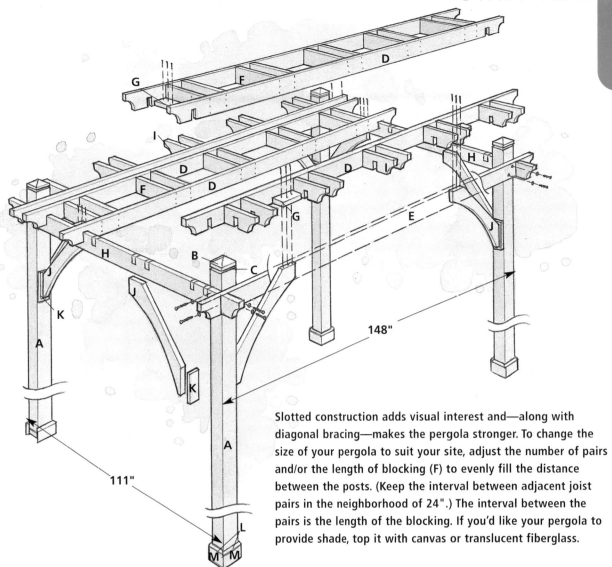

Slotted construction adds visual interest and—along with diagonal bracing—makes the pergola stronger. To change the size of your pergola to suit your site, adjust the number of pairs and/or the length of blocking (F) to evenly fill the distance between the posts. (Keep the interval between adjacent joist pairs in the neighborhood of 24".) The interval between the pairs is the length of the blocking. If you'd like your pergola to provide shade, top it with canvas or translucent fiberglass.

MAIN JOIST ASSEMBLY

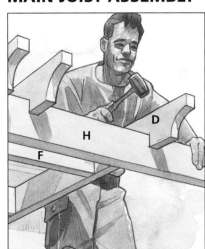

Position the main joist/blocking assemblies (D/F), slipping the main joist notches over the end girders. Fasten with screws.

BRACKET ASSEMBLY

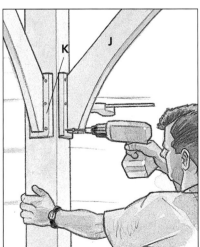

Screw the lower bracket cleats (K) to the brackets (J). Screw the bracket assemblies to the posts and the upper bracket cleats (G).

BASE TRIM ASSEMBLY

Miter-cut the base trim (M) to fit around the post bases. Apply construction adhesive and strap-clamp. Top with a cove cap (L).

CHAPTER HIGHLIGHTS

Climbing plants bring your trellis, arbor,

or pergola to life with lush foliage and

beautiful flowers. Many produce fresh

fruits or vegetables as a bonus.

This chapter introduces you to the

wide range of plants available to

get your garden looking up.

PLANTS TO GROW ON STRUCTURES

Even if your garden space is limited, there's usually room to grow upward.

Vigorous vines and climbing roses are determined to reach for the sky, and they'll quickly cover a trellis or arbor for you. What's more, they provide a wealth of color and most of them demand only minimal care.

For almost instant garden gratification, choose a flowering annual vine such as sweet pea or morning glory. Consider different effects from year to year. For longevity, plant a perennial vine. A glamorous flowering perennial such as wisteria softens the architectural lines of garden structures and offers shade and privacy. Smaller perennials, such as clematis, add graceful, colorful accents. Ivies delight with their berries and fall foliage. Climbing roses, prized for their exuberant (and often fragrant) flowers, can turn an unsightly garden corner into a spectacular scene. Remember edibles too. Grapes, tomatoes, and more grow on vines.

This chapter will help you decide which climbing plants are right for your garden.

Reach for the Sky

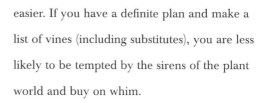

Strolling through a local nursery, leafing through a catalog, or browsing an Internet plant site is an inspiring—but often overwhelming—experience. How do you decide what to buy?

Jotting down a list makes your shopping easier. If you have a definite plan and make a list of vines (including substitutes), you are less likely to be tempted by the sirens of the plant world and buy on whim.

Begin with the basics: Evaluate your garden and decide what you want to accomplish for a particular area. The possibilities narrow down automatically as you go through the site conditions. Consider your hardiness zone; the amount of sun and shade the area receives daily; the orientation of the area to the sun (north-, south-, east-, or west-facing); the soil type (sandy, clay, or loam); the drainage; the air movement; and accessibility to water and the garden.

It's relatively easy to improve garden soil or make adjustments for drainage, but you'll enjoy more success if you try to work with, rather than against, existing sun and shade conditions. For example, a south-facing site in Zone 6 that receives full sun would be a good location for a climbing rose. A Virginia creeper or Boston ivy will fare better in a shady or partial-sun spot and will endure a harsh winter.

Here are some tips for buying plants at nurseries and home and garden centers, from mail-order catalogs, and on the Internet:

■ **Nurseries:** Usually the most expensive option, but plants are generally well cared for and free of pests and disease. Most nurseries sell

▼ Bougainvillea is showy in bloom and gives shade. It grows best in Zones 9–10

plants that are tailored to grow in your area and replace plants for free if they die within the first year. Plants are usually sold in containers; you don't need to plant them immediately.

■ **Home and garden centers:** Read plant tags carefully to ensure that plants offered are within your hardiness range. Prices are usually lower than at nurseries, but employees may not know as much about plant care or maintenance. Plants may be stressed from lack of water or from insect damage.

■ **Mail-order catalogs:** From general-interest to specialty plants, catalogs have the widest variety of plants, sizes, and prices. Plants are often delivered bare-root and must be planted immediately. The plant you want may be out of stock, so have a backup in mind.

■ **Internet:** This is the most convenient for ordering and comparison shopping. Most websites allow you to instantly know whether the plant you want is in or out of stock. Plants usually arrive bare-root.

▲ Concord is one of many grape varieties suitable for growing on arbors and pergolas.

▶ The spectacular passionflower blossom lends an exotic aura to any garden. The perennial vine grows to 20 feet and is hardy in Zones 7–10.

◀ Climbing roses like the 'Polka' variety, bring beautiful colors to the garden. (See pages 124–125.)

GALLERY OF CLIMBING PLANTS

Here's a look at some garden-worthy and readily available annual, evergreen, and perennial vines.

BOSTON IVY

Parthenocissus tricuspidata

Deciduous perennial

If you want a pretty, glossy, fast-growing green vine for sun or shade, try this native woodland plant. It climbs up to 50 feet, depending on the species, and supports itself by attaching via twining and aerial tendrils. It produces insignificant flowers in summer followed by dark blue berries in fall, which birds feast upon. Foliage turns bright crimson in full sun. Grows best in Zones 4–8. (Boston ivy's country cousin, Virginia creeper, thrives in Zones 3–9.) Comments: A tough vine, surviving poor soils, pollution, salt spray, and other difficult conditions with ease. (Shown *below*)

CLEMATIS

Clematis spp. (Large-flowered hybrids)

Deciduous perennial

This popular vine climbs a manageable 8 to 12 feet and produces showy large flowers in purple, white, pink, red, and blue that range in size from just a few inches to as large as dinner plates, depending on the cultivar. Even the ripened flower heads are pretty, creating lovely silky whirls after the blooms are gone. Choose the right cultivar and you'll have a clematis that will bloom from early summer into fall. Other cultivars bloom twice, once in early summer and again in late summer or early fall. Try *C. ×Jackmanii* for violet flowers, 'Candida' for white, or 'Nelly Moser' for pinkish blooms. Grows best in Zones 4–8 Comments: Needs rich, well-drained soil with plentiful moisture and sunlight (partial shade in warmer climates). Plant so that roots are in shade and leaves are exposed to sun. (Shown *above*)

CLIMBING HYDRANGEA

Hydrangea petiolaris
Deciduous perennial

Produces white, lacy, slightly fragrant flower clusters in late spring. In fall the leaves often turn vivid yellow before falling away, revealing attractive reddish-brown bark. Grows best in Zones 5–7.

Comments: Likes a bit of shade and good moisture and drainage. Grows slowly at first, often taking several years to produce flowers, but then takes off. (Shown *above*)

ENGLISH IVY

Hedera helix
Evergreen

A classic, climbing up to 50 feet, depending on conditions and the cultivar. It attaches itself to surfaces with tiny holdfasts and produces glossy green or green-variegated three- to five-lobed leaves. 'Baltica,' 'Bulgaria,' 'Ogallala,' 'Romania,' and 'Thorndale' are cold hardy

varieties that can handle Zone 5 winters. Grows best in Zones 6–9.

Comments: Grows in sun or shade and tolerates drought.

MOONFLOWER

Ipomoea alba
Annual

The night-blooming cousin of the more commonly grown morning glory, moonflower has the same heart-shape leaves and wonderful spiraling trumpet-shape flowers. It gets its name from its habit of opening in late afternoon or on cloudy days. When open, the flowers are richly fragrant and attractive to night-flying moths, including the fascinating hummingbird moth. Planted from seed in spring, it rapidly climbs 8 to 10 feet and blooms from midsummer to frost. Comments: Plant in full sun in average to poor soil. Do not overfertilize or you'll have enormously tall vines and very few flowers. Moonflower often grows as a perennial in Zones 9–11.

◀ Leaves of different ivies are distinctive.

COMPANION PLANTS

MORNING GLORY

Ipomoea tricolor

Annual

Interplant this vine in average to poor soil with moonflower (*Ipomoea alba*), which will bloom in the evenings after the morning glory closes. A cottage garden classic, morning glories twine obligingly and quickly up nearly any vertical surface. They're great for arbors, trellises, and other supports that will take their height of 6 feet or more. 'Heavenly blue' is the most popular morning glory, but other species and cultivars have also become popular, especially those blooming in reds and pinks. Some other species can be somewhat invasive in the garden, however, reseeding so freely as to become a nuisance. If this happens, don't replant the following year.

Comments: Many morning glories attract hummingbirds. (Shown *above*)

SWEET PEA

Lathyrus odoratus

Annual

Prized for their pretty, intensely fragrant flowers, most sweet peas are grown as cool-season annual vines, reaching 4 to 6 feet tall. Plants produce lovely clusters of 1-inch-long, pea-type flowers in white, light orange, yellow, lavender, blue, red, or purple; some produce two-color flowers. Longer-stemmed types make classic cut flowers. Attractive gray-green leaves nicely complement these blossoms. Bloom time depends on the variety, with many blooming in early winter in mild climates and early spring to midsummer elsewhere. 'Royal family' is one of the more heat-tolerant and fragrant cultivars.

Comments: Prefers fertile, well-drained soil with a little lime. Fertilize and water well. (Shown *below*)

TRUMPET HONEYSUCKLE

Lonicera sempervirens

Deciduous perennial

This twining vine grows moderately fast, reaching 10 to 15 feet. Blooms best in the sun. Honeysuckle has the longest blooming season of the hardy climbers—the tubular flowers last from midspring until heavy frost. Grows best in Zones 4–9.

Comments: Requires average moisture; avoid drought. Susceptible to aphid attack in spring but may outgrow the insects by summer. If not, horticultural oil or insecticides are effective. Avoid Japanese honeysuckle (*Lonicera japonica*), an aggressive, weedy vine.

TRUMPET VINE

Campsis radicans

Deciduous perennial

This vine grows quickly, reaching 20 to 40 feet in just three or four years, and attaches itself with aggressive twining and aerial rootlets. Its size means it must be sited carefully, so be sure to provide ample support with a large arbor. Its rootlets and vigorous twining can be damaging to wood, shingles, and loose masonry. It's a tough plant, tolerating urban shade and pollution, yet its delicate scarlet-orange, tube-shaped flowers attract tiny hummingbirds. Flourishes in full sun to partial shade. Grows best in Zones 4–9.

Comments: Plant established plants in spring or fall. Do not fertilize. Trumpet vine blooms on new wood, so prune heavily each spring for best flowering and to control size. Cut out suckers at its base. (Shown *left*)

WISTERIA

Wisteria spp.

Perennial

If you have the space and a large, heavy-duty support, such as a large arbor, this Japanese native will reward you with wonderfully romantic, fragrant 1- to 2-foot-long dripping flower clusters in mid to late spring. Within just a few years, this vigorous vine can reach 100 feet, depending on the variety. It has a heavy trunk that resembles that of a small tree and can, in fact, smother a small tree planted next to it. Its twining branches can pry off wooden siding or lift roof shingles, so site it carefully. Root suckers may be invasive. Well-placed and tended, however, it will reward you for many years with gorgeous flowers in purple, pink, rose, or white. Grows best in Zones 5–9.

Comments: These long-lived vines need full sun and can grow 15 feet per year. New wisterias, however, may not bloom for the first 5 to 10 years. Prune frequently to keep in desired boundaries. (Shown *above*)

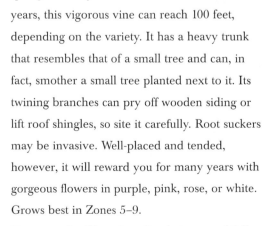

GALLERY OF CLIMBING ROSES

Climbing roses add romance and bright color to any garden.

When planted in full sun and trained to a trellis, pergola, or arbor, climbers bring their flowers to eye level where you can enjoy them. They're easy to grow as long as you choose the right one for your climate and site. Climbers usually reach a mature width of about 4 feet, and canes can reach to 10 feet or more. Some bloom just once; others bloom sporadically until frost. Fragrance varies by cultivar.

'ALOHA'

Climbing hybrid tea, medium pink

A shapely and elegant plant with a sweet rose fragrance, blooms are rose-pink on the front, darker on the reverse. Canes reach 6 to 10 feet in an upright habit. Grows best in Zones 3–9.

Comments: One of the few climbing hybrid teas for which there is no bush form.

'BLAZE'

Climber, medium red

Produces a summer-long abundance of solid scarlet red flowers (20 to 25 petals) in large clusters on strong stems all along the length of its thick canes. Blooms have a light tea fragrance. Canes grow to 12 to 14 feet long. Grows best in Zones 5–10.

Comments: Train canes early to horizontal positions at various heights. (Shown *above right*)

'CANDY CANE'

Climbing miniature, pink blend

This popular little climber features dashing semidouble blooms (13 to 15 petals) that are striped deep pink and pure white. Massive clusters with up to 20 blooms often arch on canes to form a candy-cane shape. Sprays may last for several weeks. Pliable 4- to 6-foot canes make training on supports easy. Zones 5–11.

Comments: Remove spent flowers to improve repeat bloom cycle. (Shown *left*)

'HIGH HOPES'

Climber, medium pink

Features a true rose-pink color, rare among climbers. The buds are elegant, long, and pointed, opening to perfectly formed, high-centered blooms that exude the sweet scent of strawberries. Canes are often 10 to 12 feet long, ideal for training on an arbor or pergola. Grows best in Zones 5–10.

Comments: Very winter-hardy and disease-resistant. (Shown *left*)

'POLKA'

Climber, apricot blend

These large, fluffy, old-fashioned flowers (30 to 35 petals) grow onto a stem or in small clusters on strong stems. Color is a dramatic copper-salmon, fading to light salmon pink with deep copper centers. Fragrance is strong and pervading. Plants reach 10 to 12 feet in most climates, with healthy-looking dark green foliage.

Grows best in Zones 5–10.

Comments: Ideal variety for cut flowers.

▼ 'John Cabot' rose bears small clusters of red to dark orchid-pink blooms all summer. It winters without protection. Zones 3–10.

Comments: Spent blooms naturally fall away, initiating the next bloom cycle and keeping the bush tidy.

'JOSEPH'S COAT'

Climber, red blend

Hues range through red, pink, orange, and yellow in abundant flower clusters with a light tea scent. Foliage is glossy apple green. Canes average 8 to 10 feet long. Grows best in Zones 5–10.

Comments: Provide protection in harsh winter climates.

'NEW DAWN'

Climber, light pink

Large, full, cameo pink flowers (40 to 45 petals) with sweet rose bouquet appear all summer in small clusters (sometimes one bloom per stem). Canes can reach 12 to 20 feet. Grows best in Zones 4–10.

PRUNING VINES AND CLIMBING ROSES

The rule for pruning vines and climbing roses is similar to the one for all plants: Know the plant and its needs. Think about what you're trying to accomplish. Are you pruning to rejuvenate an old plant, to shape the plant, to encourage flowering or fruiting, or to control size and shape?

The good news about annual vines is that they rarely need pruning, because their life cycles last just one season. To extend blooming, snip off flowers as soon as they fade.

Here are some general practices to follow when pruning perennial vines:

Make your cut just above a healthy bud or at the juncture of two stems. Angle the cut down and away from the bud at a 45-degree angle so that sap will drip away from the cut. New growth will appear from this bud. Cuts made toward the end of a stem encourage new shoots to emerge along its length and promote a look of fullness.

▼ **Removing all the side shoots—called *cutting back to the bones*—reduces the size of the vine and controls its growth while keeping the plant's shape.**

▲ To drastically control growth or rejuvenate a vine, prune it to 1 foot above the ground.

Removing stems to the trunk tends to redirect growth to the top of the vine. You can also cut most perennials back to ground level if you need to drastically control growth or rejuvenate a plant that's grown old. New growth will be well-branched and vigorous.

Removing shoots is often the most challenging part of vine maintenance. They are usually entwined among themselves and the trellis or arbor. Don't try to yank out a long, entangled shoot. You may damage other parts of the vine and the support. Try cutting a stem from the top, removing small sections at a time. Continue until the entire stem is gone.

◀ Pruning requires few tools, so buy good ones. Sharp tools make better cuts, which heal more quickly and promote plant health.

Pruning is good therapy for plants and gardeners. Just be sure to buy a good pair of scissor-type pruning shears and work gloves. While pruning, step back from time to time to assess your progress; don't get carried away. Because of their vitality, most vines and climbing roses are forgiving of pruning mistakes and quick to recover.

▼ Wear heavy gloves when you prune roses or other barbed vines. Lighter gloves will work fine for less-prickly plants.

When to prune depends on your goal. If you're trying to maximize blooms, prune vines after they flower. In general, prune spring bloomers in early summer and summer bloomers in winter. This allows them time to produce buds for next year's bloom.

Winter is a good time to prune deciduous vines. With the foliage gone, you can see the basic structure of the vine, and the cut stems are easier to remove.

Climbing and rambling roses bloom on old wood, so they should not be severely pruned in winter, unless you need to remove crowded or diseased shoots. Prune once-blooming varieties after they flower. Prune repeat bloomers while they are dormant, ideally in early spring before the final frost date for your region.

CHAPTER HIGHLIGHTS

BUILDING BASICS

No one is born with the ability to hit every nail squarely and saw every line arrow-straight. So it's no excuse to say, "I'm just not handy."

Everyone starts out with no manual dexterity whatsoever, then gradually develops hundreds of skills that use hand-eye coordination—everything from grasping a rattle to driving a car.

This chapter debunks the myth of unhandiness. The following pages show some tools, techniques, and materials you can master to become an accomplished do-it-yourselfer.

Even if you've successfully accomplished a few indoor do-it-yourself projects, such as installing shelves or building fine furniture, you'll find this chapter helpful because there are important differences between indoor and outdoor projects. You use most of the same tools, to be sure, but outdoor projects often call for different lumber, fasteners, and finishes. They may require different construction techniques too.

Master these building basics and you can construct any of the projects featured in Chapter 2, along with just about any other outdoor structure you can dream up on your own.

Landscaping Tools

The landscaping tools you'll need for trellis, arbor, and pergola projects depend largely on the project you're taking on, but before you start you should have on hand at least some of the implements shown here. Here's what each of them does:

Drain spade. With its narrow, pointed blade, a drain spade is ideal for digging trenches. It also comes in handy in other tight spots, such as shoveling dirt or concrete around posts that you're setting.

Hand auger. You screw this one into the ground to bore holes for posts. Give it a turn, lift it out of the hole, knock dirt off the blades, and repeat the process until you've reached the depth you want. Or rent a power version like one of those in the sidebar *opposite*.

Clamshell posthole digger. A pair of long-handled shovels hinged together offers another way to dig postholes. You open the shovel blades, jam them into the ground, separate the handles and lift out a chunk of earth. (You may need to rotate the blades back and forth to cut roots or dislodge small rocks.)

Round-blade shovel. Use this workhorse for all sorts of digging jobs. A long-handled version provides better leverage in excavations more than a foot deep. A square-blade spade (not shown) is best for digging up sod and knifing through tree roots.

Drain spade

Hand auger

Clamshell posthole digger

Iron rake

Round-blade shovel

Tamper

Trowel

Iron rake. Also known as a bow rake, an iron rake breaks up and levels soil. You can also do these jobs, and mix concrete, with a garden hoe (not shown).

Tamper. Compact soil around posts and in other spots that require firm, dense earth. You can make your own tamper by nailing a 12-inch plywood square to one end of a length of 2×4.

Trowel. Move small amounts of soil in tight spots with this basic gardener's tool. It also comes in handy for mixing concrete and placing it around posts.

Buying tips

Examine tools before you buy. If a handle is too long, short, or heavy for you, try another. Check connections. The best spades, shovels, and rakes have a metal shank extending partway up the handle for additional strength. Trowels are more durable when they have wooden handles driven into a metal shank.

Remember that most manufacturers offer several lines of tools at various price levels. You might decide on an inexpensive version of an item you'll use only a few times, but spend more to buy high-quality tools you'll use often.

Caring for landscaping tools

Well-made tools last for years if you don't abuse or neglect them. Here are some maintenance hints:
■ Clean tools after each use with a paint stick or steel brush to keep soil from encrusting.
■ Wipe wooden handles with linseed oil. Paint them a bright color if you tend to lose tools.
■ Sharpen tools for efficiency and safety. Follow instructions that come with each tool. Usually you can do the job with a metal file.

■ Check and tighten bolts and screws regularly.
■ For safety and to maintain cutting edges, hang tools on the wall of your garage or shed. Protect steel blades against rust by applying oil or petroleum jelly.

POWER POSTHOLE DIGGERS

If you have several postholes to dig, consider renting one of these gasoline-powered machines. Power augers come with interchangeable spiral boring bits for making holes 6, 8, or 10 inches in diameter. They can excavate holes up to 44 inches deep. Some models, like the one *above right*, can be operated by one person. The larger auger, *above left*, takes two people to operate but is less likely to kick out of a hole when it hits a rock or tree root.

■ To dig with a power auger, mark the depth of the posthole on the bit with tape and set the auger over the spot you've selected. Start the engine, adjust the speed with a handle-mounted throttle, and exert even downward pressure. After digging a few inches, slowly raise the bit to dislodge dirt from the hole.

Layout and Measuring Tools

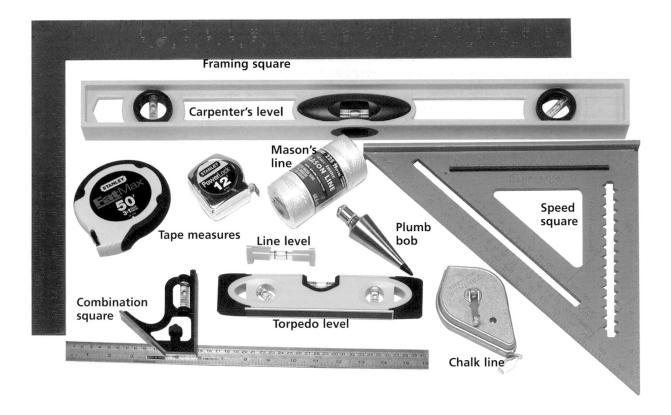

Framing square

Carpenter's level

Mason's line

Speed square

Tape measures

Line level

Plumb bob

Combination square

Torpedo level

Chalk line

Almost any project requires measurements of some sort, so you may as well get into the habit of clipping a steel tape to your belt as the first step in every job.

Remember, too, that it's surprisingly easy to misread or miscalculate a dimension. Read carefully because mistaken measurements cost time and materials.

Simple linear measurements often aren't enough. In many instances, you also need to know whether something is square, level, or plumb, as explained on pages 134–135.

Making careful, accurate measurements takes time and concentration. Sometimes you have to climb a ladder or wriggle into a tight space. Sometimes, especially at first, you'll goof anyway.

The main weapons in the battle against inaccuracy

Framing square. Often called a carpenter's square, a framing square is designed for squaring almost anything. Its large size makes it ideal for squaring large structures and marking sheet material, such as plywood.

Carpenter's level. Usually measuring 24 or 30 inches long, a carpenter's level provides accuracy over broad spans. Bubbles show level, plumb, and often 45-degree angles as well. A similar tool, called a mason's level, is 4 feet long and is useful in leveling long parts, such as the top rail of a fence.

50-foot tape. If you're laying out a large project, a 50-foot or longer cloth or flexible steel tape with a locking device saves time.

12-foot tape. This one has lots of uses. You can measure lumber and other materials for cutting, lay out straight or curved parts, measure depths (as with postholes), and determine positioning. A locking feature holds the tape in position while you make your mark. Many also have decimal equivalents, nail sizes, and other useful information on the back of the tape.

Mason's line. Coupled with the line level shown below it, *opposite*, a mason's line lets you determine level over a long distance, such as between post tops. The level clips onto the line.

Plumb bob. For determining or marking plumb, use a plumb bob suspended by a cord or mason's line.

Speed square. True to its name, a speed square speeds up layout jobs. A lip along one edge butts up against the square edge of a board

so that you can draw 90- or 45-degree lines across it. And its aluminum or plastic body is an effective guide for a circular saw or jigsaw.

Torpedo level. A short torpedo level can fit where a longer level can't. Like a carpenter's level, it has vials that measure level, plumb, and 45-degree angles.

Chalk line. Use this for marking long, straight lines on large materials, such as plywood. Hook the end over a small nail at one end of the line, extend the line taut against the material, lift, and snap it to mark the line. The one shown doubles as a plumb bob.

Combination square. Square and mark boards for crosscuts with a combination square. It also may be used as a marking and depth gauge and for laying out 45-degree miter cuts. Most combination squares include a level in the sliding handle.

ELECTRONIC LEVELS

Classic bubble levels are precision instruments, but they have a few limitations. Because even mason's levels measure 4 feet or less in length, drawing a longer plumb or vertical line—on the side of a building, for example—requires sliding the level. And every time you move it, you risk inaccuracy that will compound as you progress. Electronic levels like the laser models shown here project a light beam that makes a plumb or level line on a surface that's as long or high as the surface itself. A buzzer sounds to indicate level or plumb, a handy feature if you're working in low light or in an awkward position.

MEASURING AND MARKING

SQUARING UP STOCK

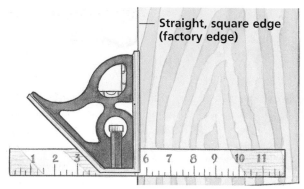
Straight, square edge (factory edge)

Before you measure, make sure the end or edge of the board you're measuring from is square. Check it with a try square or combination square, as shown. Square it up, if necessary. Measuring from an edge that isn't square leads to problems.

MARKING CUTOFF POINTS

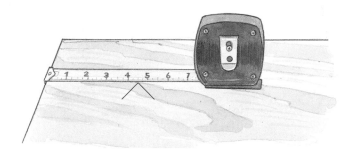

For precision, indicate your cutoff-point mark with the tip of a V-shape mark. A dot is too difficult to see; a short line might veer one way or the other. Always double-check your measurement before cutting.

MARKING CROSSCUTS

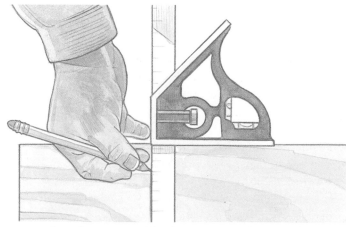

For narrow boards, use a combination square as shown to draw a fine line at the cutoff point. For wider materials, align a framing or carpenter's square to draw the cutoff line.

P recise measurements are important in every project. Learning that there is no such measurement as "about" will save you time, money, and frustration.

But be aware that not all materials are square, especially the ends of boards, dimension lumber, and timbers. Almost all materials—wood, concrete, metal, plastic—have a factory edge. A factory edge is carpenters' vernacular for the milled edge of the material, such as the planed edge of a board or the edges of a sheet of plywood. This edge usually is true, or straight, so use it as a reference point for squaring the rest of the material.

You'll need a sharp-pointed pencil to make accurate marks on your material. Carpenter's pencils, which have flat rather than round leads, work well for marking wood. For even more accuracy, use an awl, which looks like a short ice pick, or a scriber, which resembles a long steel toothpick. (Combination squares often have a scriber that stows in the square's body.)

SAW ON SCRAP SIDE

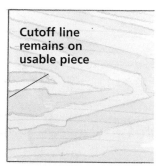
Scrap

Cutoff line remains on usable piece

Saw on the scrap side of the cutoff line, not straight down the middle of it. Otherwise, material will be cut half a saw kerf shorter than the measurement you intended. Even this small discrepancy—typically $1/16$ inch—can make a big difference.

MARKING ANGLES

▲ A combination square can mark 90- and 45-degree angles and measure depths. The blade slides through the handle to accommodate different widths. Many combination squares have plumb and level vials too.

USING A FRAMING SQUARE

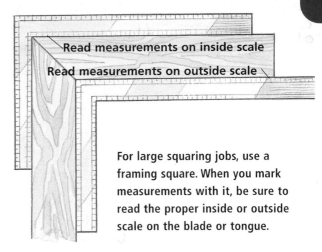

Read measurements on inside scale

Read measurements on outside scale

For large squaring jobs, use a framing square. When you mark measurements with it, be sure to read the proper inside or outside scale on the blade or tongue.

USING A POST LEVEL

A post level comes in handy for many trellis and arbor projects. It includes three vials that check for plumb on three different planes. Adjust the post until all three bubbles are centered in their vials.

USING A CARPENTER'S LEVEL

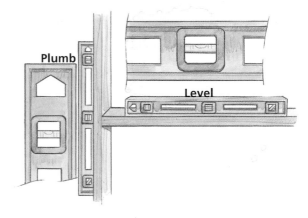

Plumb

Level

Three vials make a carpenter's level handy. You can check vials at either end to determine if a post or other vertical element is plumb. The center vial shows whether a horizontal element is level.

Using squares and levels

Square refers to an exact 90-degree angle between two surfaces. When a material is level, it's perfectly horizontal; when it's plumb, it's truly vertical.

Never assume that existing construction is square, level, or plumb. It probably isn't. To prove this to yourself, lay a level horizontally along any floor in your home, hold a level vertically against a wall section in a corner, or place a square on a door or window frame.

Don't be alarmed at the results. Variation is normal because houses and other structures settle slightly on their foundations, throwing off square, level, and plumb.

How can you check a level's accuracy? Lay it on a horizontal surface and shim it, if necessary, to get a level reading. Then turn the level end for end. If you don't get the same reading, the level needs to be adjusted or replaced. Some models allow you to calibrate the level by rotating the glass vials. Electronic levels (see page 133) come with instructions that tell how to calibrate them.

CARPENTRY HAND TOOLS

Assemble your hand-tool collection a few pieces at a time. Start with the basics, then add specialty items and power equipment as you need them. This way you're more likely to invest in quality, and as you gain proficiency, you'll also develop a clearer sense of what tools you'd like to purchase next. Which are the basics? With the assortment of tools shown here you can handle many trellis, arbor, and pergola projects. Here are descriptions of the hand tools shown:

Jack plane. Measuring 12 to 15 inches long, a jack plane makes a good general-use smoothing tool. Later you might want to add a shorter smooth plane and a block plane, which fits in the palm of your hand. A block plane with a low blade angle is good for end-grain planing.

Crosscut saw. A crosscut saw works best across the grain, the most common cutting operation. The short version shown here is called a *toolbox saw* because it's small enough to fit into a toolbox.

Ripsaw. You can use a crosscut saw to rip a board–saw with the grain–but you'll make slow headway. A ripsaw cuts best with the grain.

Miter box and backsaw. Use these for absolutely square and miter cuts in narrow lumber, such as trim pieces. The box guides the cuts; the saw–a small crosscut saw with a reinforced back–does the work. It's so named because it cuts on the back stroke.

Sanding block. Sandpaper works best when it's held flat against the surface. Buy a wood, plastic, or rubber sanding block or wrap sandpaper around a block of wood.

3-pound sledge. Sometimes called a *baby sledge*, this hefty hammer easily handles heavy-duty pounding jobs, such as driving stakes.

Curved-claw hammer. Make a 16-ounce curved-claw hammer your first tool purchase. Besides driving a vast array of fasteners, a claw hammer also pulls them.

Ripping-claw hammer. Use a 20-ounce hammer with a ripping claw for driving framing nails and prying boards apart.

Nail set. Countersink or *set* nails beneath the wood's surface with this inexpensive tool.

Screwdrivers. You'll need both straight and phillips heads for attaching hardware.

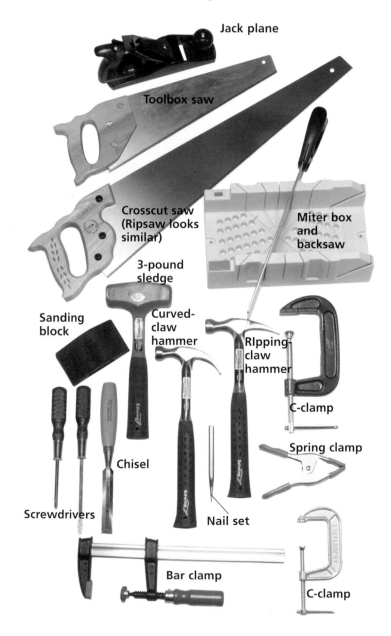

Jack plane

Toolbox saw

Crosscut saw
(Ripsaw looks similar)

Miter box and backsaw

3-pound sledge

Sanding block

Curved-claw hammer

Ripping-claw hammer

C-clamp

Spring clamp

Chisel

Screwdrivers

Nail set

Bar clamp

C-clamp

Chisels. Use a chisel when you need to cut mortises for hinges, remove excess wood from grooves and joints, shape joints, form inside and outside curves in wood, or trim wood to close tolerances. Chisels with $\frac{1}{4}$- $\frac{3}{8}$-, $\frac{1}{2}$-, and $\frac{3}{4}$-inch-wide blades, often sold in sets, will perform most chiseling chores.

Clamps. An assortment of clamps is essential for most gluing tasks and also can temporarily hold materials together while you drill, saw, screw, or nail them. C-clamps, spring clamps, and bar clamps are handy types to have.

This list of hand tools doesn't include a drill. That's because your first power-tool purchase should be a corded or cordless electric drill, which also serves as a screwdriver for outdoor projects. See pages 140–141 for power tools.

Buying tips

Take your time in deciding on any tool, and try to learn what it's made of. With metal tools, you'll encounter several different alloys.
■ **Carbon steel**, made of iron and carbon, is fine for screwdrivers and other tools that don't generate heat.
■ **Low-alloy steel** includes some tungsten or molybdenum to increase heat-resistance.
■ **High-alloy steel**, which has a much higher tungsten or molybdenum content, is the best choice for high-speed cutting tools. Power saw blades tipped with tungsten carbide will last the average do-it-yourselfer for years.
■ **Metal tools differ**, too, in the way they're made. Casting, the least expensive manufacturing technique, for instance, can result in flaws in the metal that make it liable to chip and break. If you'll be hitting or applying muscle to the tool, don't buy the cast type. A broken tool can cause serious injury.

Forged or drop-forged tools are almost indestructible, an important quality for items such as hammers and wrenches. Chisels should be made of high-quality steel with precisely ground bevels and edges.

JAPANESE PULL SAWS

These thin-blade saws cut on the pull stroke, not the push stroke like traditional Western saws. This prevents the blade from buckling and binding, providing more control. The saw can't jump out of its groove and cause damage to the project or the user's hands.

■ The thin steel makes the blade flexible, allowing the saw to adapt to specialty tasks, such as cutting dowels flush with the surrounding surface. The unique blade design works equally well for both cross and rip cutting, undercuts, and reverse cuts.

■ It's difficult to sharpen these fine-tooth saws, so most have replaceable blades. Some pull saw blades have a single cutting edge; others have teeth for ripping on one side, crosscutting on the other.

Don't overlook a tool made partly of plastic either. For instance, fiberglass handles on hammers, sledges, and axes are every bit as strong as steel shanks, yet they have even more resilience than old-fashioned wood handles and deliver less shock to your hand and arm.

USING A HAMMER AND SAW

There's a knack to using most hand tools, but it doesn't take long to acquire these basic skills. Here's what you need to know.

Using a hammer

For maximum leverage and control, hold onto the hammer near the end of the handle, not up around the neck. If you do this and concentrate on the job at hand, you'll find yourself driving nails without straining (or hitting) your arm, wrist, or hand. Always use a hammer with a face slightly larger than the nail you're striking.

Before using an unfamiliar hammer, check it for a loose, bent, or split handle. Any of these can cause injury or damage when you swing it.

Using a crosscut saw

There's a special rhythm in using any saw. It's a sort of rocking stroke that starts from the shoulder and works down through the arm and hand. Hold the saw at about 45 degrees to the work. You need to apply very little pressure in this cutting motion. In fact, your main task is to steer the blade while it does its work. If you

DRIVING NAILS

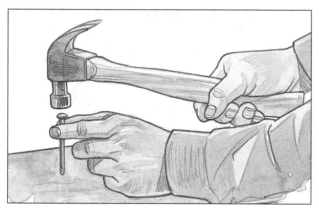

Hold the nail near its head. That way, if you miss, the hammer will glance off your fingers rather than crush them. Ask skilled carpenters how to use a hammer, and they'll show you their hands and tell you, "Carefully."

To hit a nail dead-on, keep your eye on the nail, not the hammer. Let the weight of the hammer do the work. You don't need to apply a lot of muscle to it. After a while, you'll find you can sink a nail in just three or four blows.

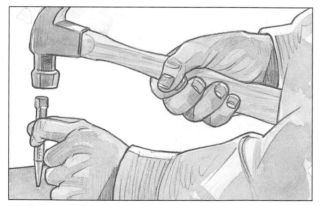

The last blow from the hammer should leave the head flush with the surface. If you want to drive it deeper, don't dimple the wood's surface. Countersink the nailhead with a nail set.

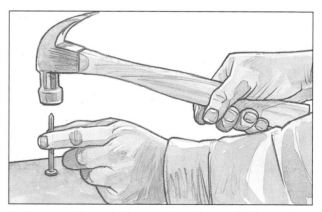

Nailing near the end of a board tends to split the wood. To avoid this problem, blunt the tip of the nail as shown or drill a pilot hole first.

SAWING BASICS

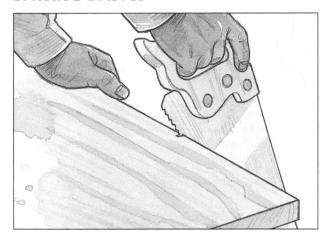

Start a handsaw in a piece of wood at the heel of the saw. The first stroke should be a gentle upstroke. This helps the saw "find" the cutoff line.

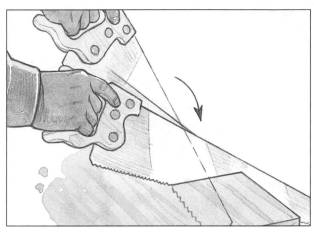

The saw stroke should rock slightly, following an arc as your arm swings from your shoulder. Let the weight of the saw do the work. Pressure won't speed up the cut.

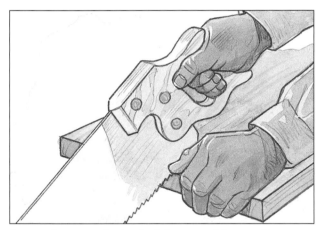

Start a ripsaw at the heel of the saw with a small upstroke, just as you would with a crosscut saw. Remember, a ripsaw cuts on the forward stroke, so relax on the pull stroke.

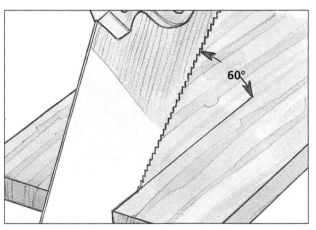

Keep the saw at a 60-degree angle to the work. You'll do this automatically with more experience. If the saw veers away from the cutting line, twist the blade slightly to steer it back.

apply pressure with your hand and forearm, the saw will wander off the cutting line or cut at an angle, and the edge won't be square.

Using a ripsaw

A ripsaw cuts wood along the length of its grain. This workhorse usually has 5½ teeth per inch set about one-third wider than the blade thickness, so it slides easily. Ripsaws cut only on the forward stroke. Use the same techniques with a ripsaw as you would with a crosscut saw. But hold a ripsaw at about a 60-degree angle to the work instead of the 45-degree angle for a crosscut saw.

With any saw, cut on the scrap side of the cutting line. You can always remove wood with a plane or rasp if your piece is a bit too long, but you can't add it if the piece is too short.

POWER TOOLS

Power tools allow you to get the job done faster and easier—and frequently more accurately as well. But don't abandon your hand tools entirely. Instead, consider power tools as extensions of your hand tools. There will be times when a hand tool will be the best tool to use.

When choosing between portable and stationary power tools, consider that portable tools are much less expensive, you can take them to the job site, and they're easier to store. Here are some top picks for portable power tools:

Drill/driver. A cordless drill/driver is the most versatile tool you can have in your tool kit. Drills for home use come with ¼-, ⅜-, and ½-inch chuck capacity. You can handle most outdoor drilling tasks with a ⅜-inch chuck.

Purchase a variable-speed drill, if possible. With these models, the motor revs up from zero to full speed, depending on how far you squeeze the trigger switch. Better drill/drivers are also reversible, which means you can remove screws as well as drive them. Get one with at least a 12-volt motor and a spare battery.

Drill bits. Drilling also requires a drill bit, basically a rotary chisel with two edges. Start with a selection of twist bits; they're usually sold in sets. Next, add ¼-, ½-, and ¾-inch spade bits for larger and deeper holes. Masonry bits drill holes in concrete, brick, and stone. Screwdriver bits drive slotted- and phillips-head screws.

Circular saw. Squeeze the trigger of a portable electric circular saw and you can feel right away that you've got a powerful cutting

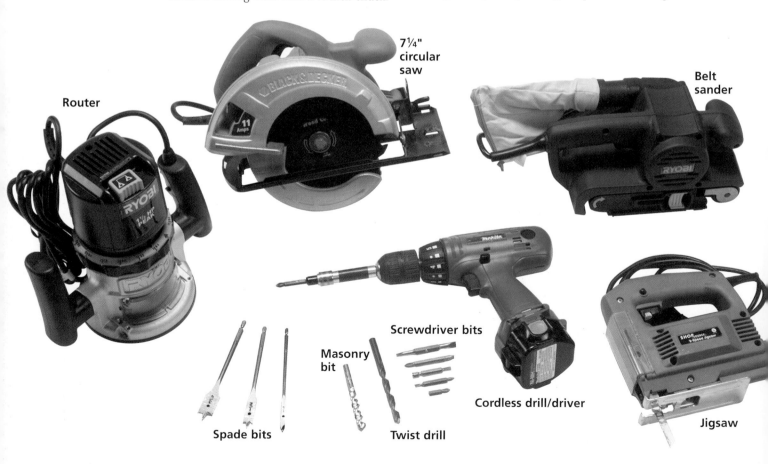

Router

7¼" circular saw

Belt sander

Spade bits

Masonry bit

Screwdriver bits

Twist drill

Cordless drill/driver

Jigsaw

machine in your hands. In fact, a circular saw can rip and crosscut materials just about as fast as you can move your arm. For most chores around the house, use a 7¼-inch model with a carbide-tipped combination blade. Be sure the one you buy has a smooth-working blade guard. The guard opens as the saw enters the wood, then snaps closed for safety after the cut is made.

Jigsaw. A lightweight jigsaw can crosscut, rip, miter, bevel, and cut curves in almost any material. Only one hand is needed to guide a jigsaw. Most cuts can be made quickly and accurately, especially if you have a rip-guide accessory. Buy a variable-speed jigsaw, a feature that lets you control the number of strokes per minute and make smooth cuts in most materials.

Belt sander. Portable electric sanders supply the sustained muscle power that you need for sanding projects. Just flip the starter switch, press down lightly, and steer. In fact, this equipment does such an efficient job of quickly removing material and smoothing, your biggest problem may be controlling the machine. A light-duty finishing or orbital sander is a good choice for smoothing interior projects. For outdoor structures, a belt sander is the tool to use. Buy or rent one, depending on how often you will use it. Make sure it has a dust bag, an attachment that catches much of the dust before it gets into the air. Most belt sanders can also be connected to a shop vacuum or dust-collection system to control dust.

Router. If not the most versatile tool made, a router certainly comes close. Basically an electric chisel, a router planes, cuts, and shapes; makes grooves, mortises, dovetails, and other joints; and trims edges off plastic laminate. It also cuts dadoes, makes pocket cuts, and much more. A router's cost depends on its features and accessories. Start with a router and two or three basic bits, along with an edge-cutting guide. As your budget allows, you can add specialty bits for fancy joints and moldings.

CORDLESS POWER TOOLS

Not to be confused with battery-operated toys, these tools now are used widely throughout the building trades. Potent batteries give these tools surprising power, often allowing you to make hundreds of cuts or holes before recharging.

■ Most models feature removable batteries that can be recharged in an hour or two. Battery sizes and voltages are not standard, however. If you think you may eventually purchase more than one cordless tool, stick to a single manufacturer and make sure all accept the same battery. This way, you can switch batteries in the middle of a job and never have to purchase expensive spares. Many manufacturers offer cost-effective sets of tools—such as a drill and a saw—with a single battery charger.

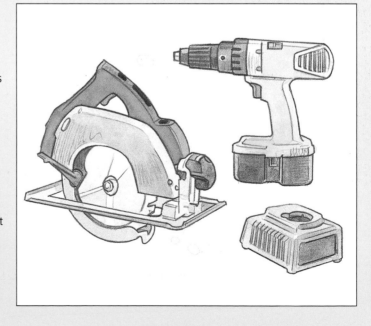

BUYING LUMBER

Some trees withstand the elements for centuries with nary a complaint. But cut one down and mill it into lumber, and it becomes vulnerable to extreme heat and cold, wind, rain, snow, ice, airborne pollutants, damaging ultraviolet radiation, insects, and more. Fortunately, some species hold up much better than others when they're made into lumber.

The heart of the matter

How well a board resists decay depends largely on what part of the tree it came from.

Heartwood, the tree's mature central core, is the toughest. You can easily identify heartwood in many species by its much deeper color.

Sapwood, which comes from the outer part of the tree, is usually lighter in color and is also a lightweight performer when it comes to strength and decay resistance. Heartwood of any species is preferable for outdoor use.

REDWOOD

Softwood choices

Once, almost everybody used redwood for outdoor projects. Back then, the stock was widely available at a reasonable price in the higher grades that showcased the wood's warm, rich, reddish brown heartwood.

High-grade redwood is not as widely available today. If it's available in your area, redwood works well for outdoor use. Cedar costs much less than redwood, and is much more widely available. Depending on where you live, you may find your lumberyard stocked with cedar native to your region, such as western red or northern white. All cedar species are moderately soft with generally straight grain and a coarse texture.

Treated lumber

Pressure-treated (PT) lumber, typically southern pine saturated with a chemical preservative, works especially well for trellises, fences, decks, and other outdoor structures. Until recently, about 90 percent of the treated wood sold for residential use was treated with chromated copper arsenate (CCA), but questions about the safety of CCA arose. The result was an agreement between manufacturers and the U.S. Environmental Protection Agency (EPA) to phase out CCA lumber by December 31, 2003.

Alternatives to CCA for lumber treatment are rapidly gaining ground. (Find out more about these on page 145.) When you shop for PT lumber, look for material certified by the American Wood Preservers' Bureau. A stamp on each board–shown opposite–tells when the wood was treated, with which chemical, and where you can use the wood for best results. Wood rated for ground contact is the best choice for posts, for instance.

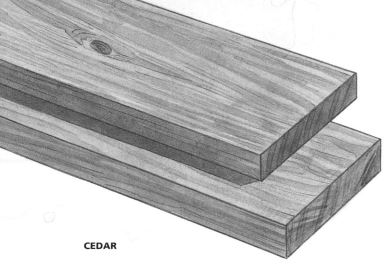

CEDAR

exterior-use hardwoods—though not available in every region—include bald cypress, honey locust, black locust, and sassafras.

TREATED LUMBER

Outdoor hardwoods

Hardwoods—domestic and imported—also work well for outdoor projects but are costly. White oak, probably the most widely available exterior-grade domestic hardwood, has closed cells that make it highly resistant to decay. Don't try to substitute red oak; its open cell structure makes it more likely to rot.

The heartwood of white oak is a grayish brown, the sapwood nearly white. Other native

Imported hardwoods give your outdoor project an exotic look at an exotic price. Popular species for outdoor use include teak, Honduran or Central American mahogany, and African mahogany (khaya).

READING A GRADE STAMP

Grade stamps at one end of a board provide important information about the lumber: its species, whether it's heartwood or sapwood, whether it has been pressure-treated (and, if so, with what chemical), and whether it's suitable for contact with the ground.

■ Plywood, marked on the back of the sheet, is rated by the American Plywood Association (APA). For outdoor projects, insist on exterior-grade plywood, which resists weathering better than interior grades, or pressure-treated material.

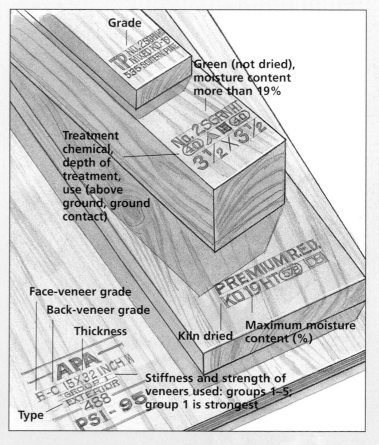

Grade

Green (not dried), moisture content more than 19%

Treatment chemical, depth of treatment, use (above ground, ground contact)

Face-veneer grade
Back-veneer grade
Thickness

Kiln dried

Maximum moisture content (%)

Stiffness and strength of veneers used: groups 1–5; group 1 is strongest

Type

MAKING A SELECTION

Wood is graded according to how many knots it has and the quality of its surface. Some lumberyards have their own grading system, but they are usually based on these and other industry-standard grades:

■ **Clear.** Has no knots.

■ **Select.** High-quality wood. Select board grades are B and better, C, and D. Select structural is the top grade in dimension lumber.

■ **No. 2 common.** Boards with tight knots and no major blemishes.

■ **No. 3 common.** Knots in these boards may be loose; board may be blemished or damaged.

■ **Standard.** Middle-grade framing lumber; good strength; used for general framing.

■ **Utility.** Economy grade used for rough framing.

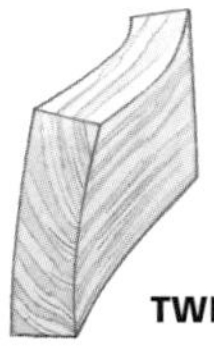

Inspecting boards

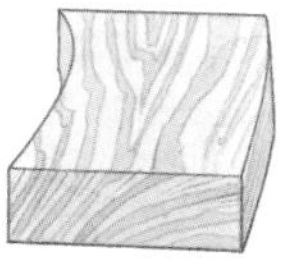

If you order lumber by telephone, you will get someone else's choice of boards, not your own. Lumberyards usually have lots of substandard wood lying around; the only way to be sure you do not get some of it is to pick out the boards yourself. Some lumberyards will not allow you to sort through the stacks because they want to keep wood neatly stacked—the best way to keep lumber from warping. But they should at least let you stand by and approve the selection. If not, confirm that you can return boards you don't like. Here are some lumber flaws to watch for:

■ A board that is heavily twisted, bowed, cupped, or crooked usually is not usable, although some bows will lie down as you nail them in place.

TWIST

BOW

LUMBER SIZES

■ **Furring.** Rough wood of small dimensions for trim, shimming, stakes, light-duty frames, latticework, and edging.

Nominal size	Actual size
1×2	¾ ×1½"
1×3	¾ ×2½"

■ **Boards.** Smooth-finished lumber for general construction, trimwork, and decking.

Nominal size	Actual size
1×4	¾ × 3½"
1×6	¾ × 5½"
1×8	¾ × 7¼"
1×10	¾ × 9¼"
1×12	¾ × 11¼"

■ **Dimension lumber.** Studs are usually 2×4, sometimes 2×6. Planks are 6 inches wide or wider. Use for structural framing, structural finishing, forming, decking, and fencing.

Nominal size	Actual size
2×2	1½ × 1½"
2×3	1½ × 2½"
2×4	1½ × 3½"
2×6	1½ × 5½"
2×8	1½ × 7¼"
2×10	1½ × 9¼"
2×12	1½ × 11¼"
4×4	3½ × 3½"
4×6	3½ × 5½"
6×6	5½ × 5½"

CUP

KNOTS

■ Knots are only a cosmetic problem unless they are loose and likely to pop out.
■ Checking, which is a rift in the surface, also is only cosmetic.
■ Splits cannot be repaired and will widen in time. Cut off split ends.

CHECKS

SPLITS

Nominal dimensions

Nominal dimensions, such as 2×4 or 1×6, are used when buying lumber. Keep in mind that the actual dimensions of the lumber will be less, as indicated in the table *opposite*. Lumber prices are often calculated by the board foot–the equivalent of a piece 12 nominal inches square and 1 nominal inch thick. Most lumberyards will not require you to calculate board feet. (To calculate board feet, multiply thickness by width, both in nominal inches, by length in feet, then divide by 12. Example: 2×4, 8 feet long: 2×4×8=64; 64/12=5.33 bd. ft.)

TREATED LUMBER TRUTHS

As noted on page 142, lumber treated with Chromated Copper Arsenate (CCA) is being phased out. Without CCA, what alternatives do you have for building lasting outdoor structures? Naturally rot- and insect-resistant woods—redwood, cedar, cypress—offer one way to go. And you can now also choose woods treated with newer, safer chemicals.

■ Alkaline (or ammoniacal) copper quaternary (ACQ) has become the leading alternative. Based on recycled copper, this treatment replaces arsenic and chromium with solutions of ammonia. ACQ-treated lumber looks similar to CCA, with a slightly more brown color.

■ Copper-azole is the newest treatment chemical. Used in Japan and Europe for some time, it is now also produced in the United States. Like ACQ, copper-azole contains no EPA-listed hazardous chemicals. In fact, azole is used to treat swimming pools and commercially grown fruit. Copper in the mix gives this lumber a greenish tint similar to ACQ or traditional CCA lumber, but copper-azole will weather to a brownish tone instead of gray.

■ You can expect to see lumber treated with either of these chemicals in lumberyards. Depending on consumer demand, you may still find CCA products there too.

Fasteners and Hardware

Just as important as the boards that go into your trellis or arbor project are the fasteners and other hardware that will hold them together. Whatever outdoor fasteners and hardware you choose, make sure they are all rustproof; they should be made of galvanized or stainless steel, brass, or other rust-resistant metal.

Nails

Once sold for so many pennies per hundred, nails today are sold by the pound. But nails still are described and sized by this old terminology; for example, a 16-penny or a 4-penny nail. To further complicate things, "penny" is indicated by the letter *d* (probably for *denarius*, Latin for *coin*). The label on the box in the hardware store identifies the size and type of nail that's inside this way: 16d common. (See the chart *opposite* to translate penny size to inches.)

Just as there are many sizes of nails, there are also many types. If you're installing plastic or metal roofing, specify roofing nails with a rubber washer under the head to seal out water. You can also buy brass, copper, stainless steel, and bronze nails. To get more holding power, select spiral, threaded, or coated types. Coated nails have a transparent, rosinlike covering that melts from the heat of friction as they are driven in, making them grip wood fibers better.

For small jobs, stay with 1-pound boxes of nails; some stores still sell them in open, bulk quantities by the pound. For most outdoor fastening jobs, you'll need common, box (same as common but thinner), and finishing nails. Also, keep an assortment of brads on hand. Brads look like miniature finishing nails; use them for molding and finishing jobs.

Screws

Screws are tough and provide exceptional holding power in wood. They're also easy to remove, making them ideal for projects you may want to disassemble later. For projects where fasteners will show, screws add a quality look that nails can't match.

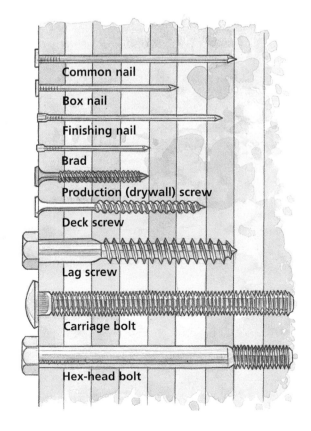

Common nail
Box nail
Finishing nail
Brad
Production (drywall) screw
Deck screw
Lag screw
Carriage bolt
Hex-head bolt

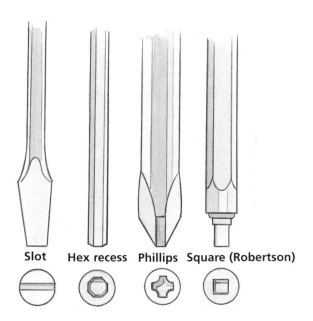

Slot   Hex recess   Phillips   Square (Robertson)

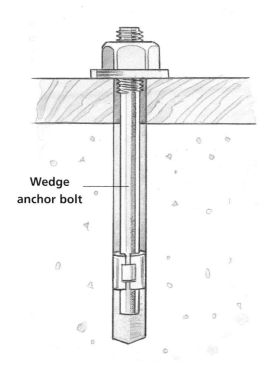

Wedge anchor bolt

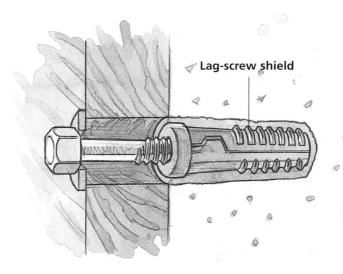

Lag-screw shield

Screw heads vary in style and slot type. Common styles are flathead, ovalhead, roundhead, and panhead. Common head types are slot, phillips, hex recess, and square.

To attach heavy objects to wood or masonry, use lag screws. These heavy-duty fasteners are good for projects with heavy framing members. Drive them into masonry using lead expansion shields like the one shown above right.

Use washers with screws to prevent the screw head from pulling into or marring the material being fastened. Some washers are decorative.

Bolts

When you need a fastener that can't pull loose yet allows you to disassemble and reassemble a joint, you're literally down to nuts and bolts. If you need to fasten two items together securely and have access to both sides of the material, a two-sided fastener like a bolt is ideal.

Bolts are sized by length and diameter. They're also classified by the number of threads per inch. For example, a ½-13×3-inch bolt is ½ inch in diameter, has 13 threads per inch, and is 3 inches long.

SIZING NAILS AND SCREWS

What size nail or screw will you need for the job? A fastener that's too small won't hold; one that's too big risks splitting the material or poking through the material to which you are fastening.

■ Use this table to convert nail pennies (d) into inches:

3d = 1¼"	4d = 1½"	6d = 2"
7d = 2¼"	8d = 2½"	10d = 3"
12d = 3¼"	16d = 3½"	20d = 4"

■ Select nails three times as long as the thickness of the material you are fastening. For instance, to attach a 1×4 (¾ inch thick), a 6d nail (2 inches long) will be a bit short. An 8d nail (2½ inches), a little more than three times the thickness of the 1×4, will do better. If that's so long it would go through the base material, use a screw.

■ Screws are sized by their length and gauge (diameter). The length of the screw, in inches, should be shorter than the thickness of the materials into which it will be driven. The smooth shank of a screw should go through the top material being fastened.

■ The gauge of screws you will need for a given project depends on the fastening strength required. Designated by number, gauges range from No. 0, which has a diameter of 1/16 inch, to No. 20, which is nearly ½ inch in diameter.

FRAMING CONNECTORS

Framing connectors–16- or 18-gauge galvanized metal brackets sized to accommodate standard dimension lumber–simplify the joining of major structural members in a trellis, arbor, or pergola. The connectors include predrilled holes through which you can drive common nails (usually 12d) or, for extra strength at critical junctures, wood screws. Some connectors come with nails or include metal prongs that you drive into the wood.

Framing connectors can be bought singly, in small packages, and in bulk–25 to 50 pieces per carton. Buying in bulk can cost half as much as buying singly or in small packages. The illustrations on these pages show some of the many types you'll find. The connectors available from your local dealer may not look exactly like the ones shown, but they make the same connections.

Post beam caps mount atop posts and include a channel that holds beams of varying dimensions. Manufacturers offer versions for both round and square posts in a variety of sizes, usually 4×4 or 6×6. (To learn about attaching post bases, see pages 164–167.)

Joist hangers attach joists to beams or headers in floor framing platforms and can reinforce almost any right-angle connection. Of course, you usually can attach a joist by simply nailing through the beam or header into the end of the joist or toenailing through the joist into the other framing member.

Multipurpose joist hangers further strengthen joist connections with angled straps that can be nailed to the tops of boards. Here again, you can save money by simply nailing or toenailing the joist in place.

Angle brackets, which come in a variety of different styles for different applications, offer yet another way to reinforce perpendicular joints. Some angle brackets attach with screws. As with joist hangers, nailing or toenailing works just as well.

Hurricane ties attach notched rafters to top plates. These expensive ties are basically designed for framing that will withstand a lot of stress, such as where hurricanes, tornadoes, and earthquakes occur and where building codes often require them.

POST BEAM CAP

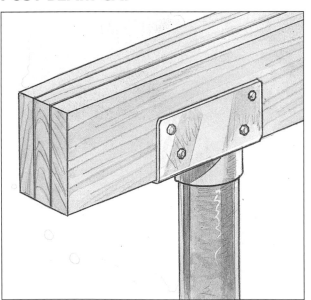

JOIST HANGER

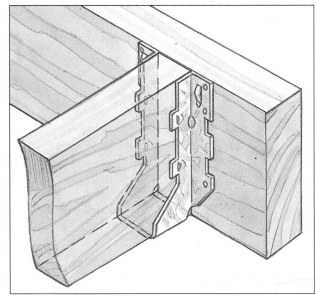

MULTIPURPOSE JOIST HANGER

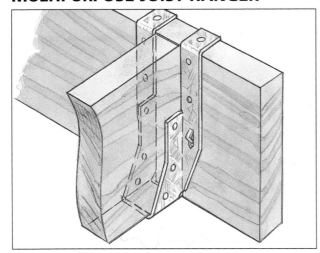

ANGLE BRACKET

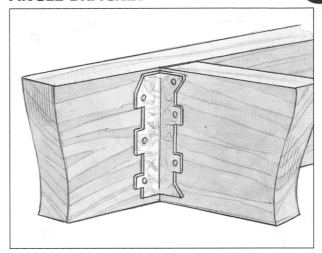

RAFTER HURRICANE TIE

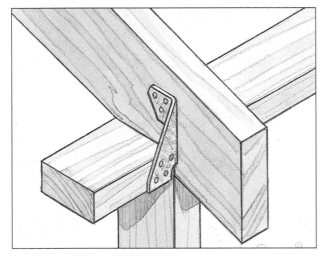

RAFTER HURRICANE TIE

Do you really need framing connectors?
Unless you live where severe weather occurs, you probably don't need them for small garden structures. Conventional joinery techniques can do the same jobs, as you'll see on the pages that follow. Connectors can speed a project along by making strong joints quickly, so they may be worth the cost—especially if their utilitarian appearance isn't noticeable or objectionable.

RAFTER HURRICANE TIE

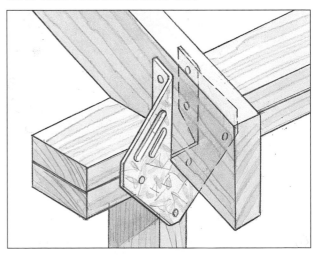

JOINERY AND CARPENTRY

A compendium of cuts

There's more than one way to saw a board. The illustrations here show eight common cuts but don't include several others that you probably won't need for a trellis or arbor project. The first few cuts shown are basic ones you can make with a handsaw. Others shown usually call for portable or stationary power tools.

■ Crosscuts move across the grain.

Since few boards come from the lumberyard in exactly the length you need, just about every project requires at least a few crosscuts, and some need dozens. You can easily crosscut with a handsaw (see page 139). For more speed and precision, use a handheld circular saw, a power mitersaw, a stationary tablesaw, or a radial-arm saw.

Crosscut

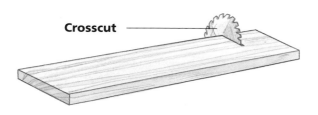

■ Rip cuts go with the grain. You'll need

to rip-cut if you want a board that's narrower than standard lumber sizes. Here again, a handsaw works fine (page 139); power saws—handheld or stationary—make faster, more accurate cuts. Most projects require at least a few rip cuts.

Rip cut

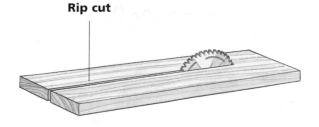

■ Miter cuts run at an angle, usually 45 degrees, across the grain. Miter cuts

are simply angled crosscuts, and you can make many of them with a crosscut saw. A miter box (page 136) improves accuracy, as will any power saw. To make a right-angle miter joint, you'll need two boards with 45-degree miter cuts.

Miter cut

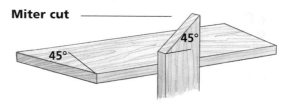

■ Bevel cuts, often at a 45-degree angle, can run with or across the grain.

You can make bevels with a handsaw, but you'll need a good eye and a steady hand to cut a bevel that's true from end to end. Power saws, especially tablesaws and radial-arm saws, work much better. As with miter cuts, a corner joint will require two bevel cuts.

Bevel

Chamfer

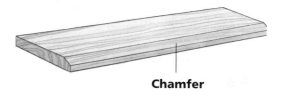

■ Chamfers can run with or across the grain. A chamfer amounts to a partial bevel

and is most often used to give a project a decorative edge. A power saw, plane, and router are the best tools for making a chamfer.

■ **Rabbet cuts can run along an edge or across the end of a board.** With care, you can crosscut a rabbet with a handsaw, but you'll need a power saw or router to make one accurately that runs lengthwise along a board. Use wide rabbet cuts to create half-lap joints, shown on page 153.

Rabbet

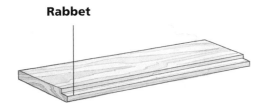

■ **Dado cuts run across the grain.** The traditional way to cut a dado is to cut the sides with a handsaw and chisel out the center. A power saw and chisel (or a tablesaw with a dado cutter) or router will do a better job much more quickly. Dado cuts require precision because they usually need to snugly accommodate the end or edge of another project part.

Dado

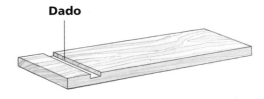

■ **Plow or groove cuts amount to dadoes that run with the grain.** You'll need a portable or stationary power saw or a router for this one. As with dado cuts, precision is the key to successful joinery.

Plow or groove

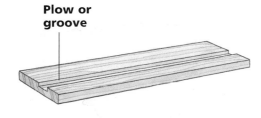

MAKING CURVED CUTS

When you want to add a curve to your trellis or arbor, use a coping saw or a handheld power jigsaw.

■ Use the coping saw for intricate cutting or scrollwork in thin materials. This hand tool allows you to set the blade in any direction in relation to its frame. To begin a cut from the inside of a board, remove the blade from the saw frame and reinstall it through a starter hole. For delicate cuts, install the blade with the teeth angled toward the handle so that the saw cuts on the back stroke.

■ Most contour cuts require a jigsaw. When you get the knack of using this tool, you can cut curves that are as smooth as any line you can draw. Turn the saw on, then begin the cut. Guide the saw slowly, without forcing the blade. If you wander from the line, don't try to make a correction with a sharp turn. Instead, guide the blade gently back to the line, or back up and start again.

BASIC WOODWORKING JOINTS

Strong wood joints are essential to all carpentry and woodworking projects. It helps if the joints look good too. Here are some of the simplest and strongest joinery methods. Each of these joints can be made with hand tools, but if you have shop tools such as a tablesaw, router, or power mitersaw, the job will go faster and the joint will be tighter. None of the joints requires cabinetmaking expertise.

Butt joints

All of the joints shown on this page are butt joints: two square-cut pieces joined together by placing the end of one member against the face or edge of another member. Of all wood joinery techniques, the butt joint is the easiest to make. Unfortunately, it's also one of the weakest. If a butt joint will be subjected to lateral stress or tension, be sure to reinforce it in some way. Reinforcement devices include corner braces, T-plates, dowels, plywood gussets, and wood cleats, all shown *below*.

However, you don't have to reinforce butt joints that bear only vertical loads, such as posts supporting a beam.

When making a butt joint, make sure the surfaces you're joining are square. Trim lumber ends with a saw, if necessary. For a strong joint, apply glue to both surfaces and nail or screw the materials together. Then add the reinforcement.

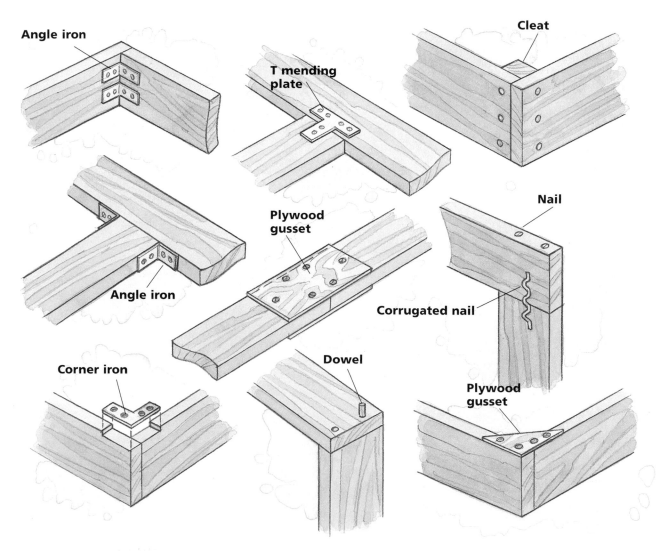

Angle iron

T mending plate

Cleat

Angle iron

Plywood gusset

Nail

Corrugated nail

Corner iron

Dowel

Plywood gusset

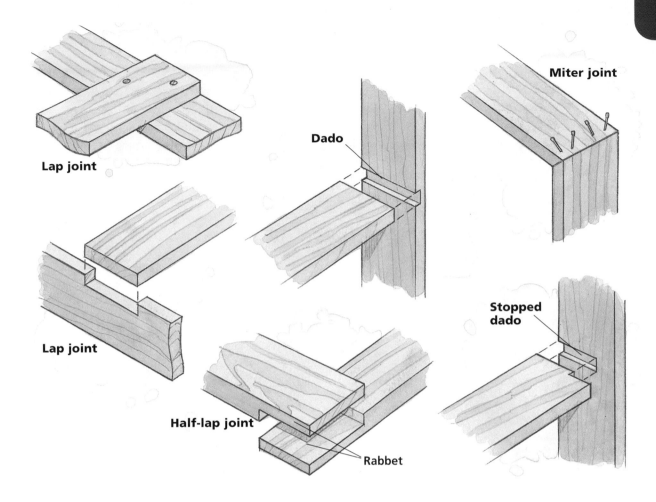

Miter joint

Lap joint

Dado

Lap joint

Stopped dado

Half-lap joint

Rabbet

Lap joints

Lap joints are stronger than butt joints and often look better as well. To make a lap joint, simply lay one of the members on top of the other and nail or screw it in place.

For a lap joint on an edge, cut a notch into one member that is as deep as the second piece is thick. Glue and clamp the two pieces together, adding fasteners if you prefer.

To make a half-lap joint, rabbet each member to half its thickness, then glue, clamp, and add fasteners. The half lap is the strongest lap joint.

Dado joints

Dado joints are attractive and strong, but they're difficult to make because you must cut a dado across one member to hold the other. A stopped dado has the same strength and hides the joint.

Miter joints

For a finished-looking corner, make a miter joint. Cut the pieces at the same angle (45 degrees for a 90-degree corner), then glue the joint and drive in finishing nails at opposing angles. A miter joint is weak, so reinforce it with metal angles, gussets, or mending plates. If you think these add-ons will mar the appearance of the project, use splines or dowels to fortify the joint more discreetly.

FASTENING WITH NAILS

Nailing mistakes that mar the wood make a job look amateurish and shoddy. All your careful measuring and cutting will be wasted if the wood ends up with a bent-over nail or "smiles" and "frowns" made by a hammer that missed the nail entirely.

Professional carpenters make nailing look easy because, when properly done, driving a nail home is not a struggle; it's done with a smooth, fluid motion. You may never be as fast at nailing as a professional because the pro gets plenty of practice, but you can learn to drive in nails accurately without damaging the material or yourself. Here's how to do it.

Set the nail

Practice on scrap pieces before you pound nails into finished work. To ensure that the hammer strikes the nail and not your fingers and that the nail will be driven into the board squarely, grasp the nail near its head and the hammer near the end of the handle. Lightly tap the nail until it stands by itself.

FACENAILING

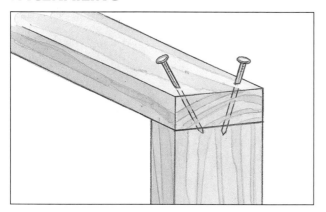

Skew nails to give them more holding power, especially in end grain. Drive in one nail at a 60-degree angle in one direction, then drive in another nail in the opposite direction. Skewed nails make it difficult for the board to pull loose.

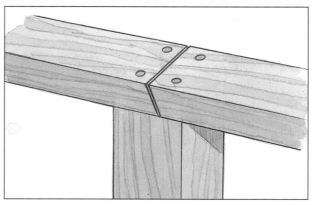

When two framing members meet atop another, like the two 2×4s and the 4×4 post shown, cut the two members to meet at the middle of the third. Drive two nails into each end. Miter-cut ends add visual interest for exposed framing.

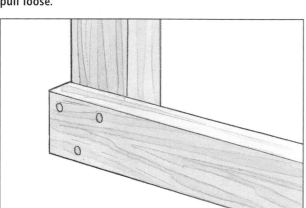

Stagger nails to avoid splits. The idea is to avoid driving neighboring nails into the same grain line; two nails will stress the grain twice as much as one nail. Three nails are in different grain lines here.

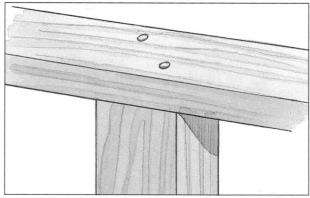

Drive two nails to attach one framing member to another, as shown. Using more nails than you need won't make the joint stronger and could split the wood.

TOENAILING

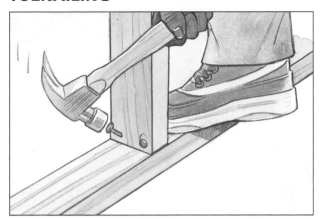

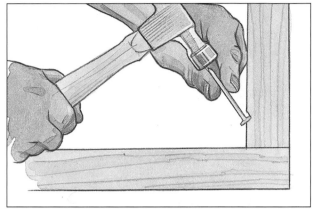

Toenailing, driving nails at an angle through one piece into another, takes some practice. Brace the part you're nailing through with your foot and drive nails at a 45-degree angle into the other part.

Tap the nail until its point bites into the wood. If you have difficulty toenailing, drill pilot holes for the nails or make a depression for the nail by tapping the head into the wood, as shown *above*.

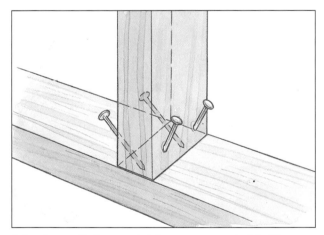

Drive four nails into each joint, two on each side. The first nail may move the vertical piece, but the second nail, driven from the other side, will move it back into position.

To toenail into vertical members, hold the nail at a steep angle, tap it once or twice, then reduce the angle to 45 degrees as you drive the nail home.

Drive the nail home

Once the nail is set in place, remove your hand from it. Keep your eye on the nail as you swing the hammer, letting the weight of the hammerhead do the driving.

Beginners tend to hold a hammer stiffly and keep their shoulders stiff, swinging from the elbow. This leads to a tired, sore arm and to mistakes. Loosen up. Your whole arm should move as you swing from the shoulder. Keep your wrist loose so the hammer can give a final snap at the end of each blow. The entire motion should be relaxed and smooth.

With the last hammer blow, push the head of the nail flush or nearly flush with the surface of the wood. The convex shape of the hammer face allows you to do this without marring the surface of the wood around the head. Let the head of a finishing nail or brad sit slightly above the surface, then drive it home with a nail set.

DRIVING SCREWS

Screw threads grip wood fibers in a way that a smooth nail cannot. When a screw is driven home, the threads exert tremendous pressure against the screw head to hold the fastener firmly in place. With the right tools, driving screws can be almost as quick as nailing. If you make a mistake, it's easy to remove a screw without damaging your work. Screws must be driven with care, however. Start straight; there is no way to correct a crooked start as you drive the screw. Drill a pilot hole, or the screw may split the wood and not hold. If the pilot hole is too large, the screw will not grip well.

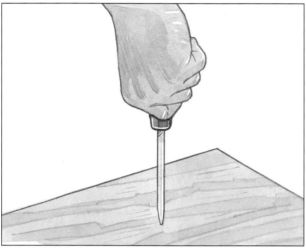

Make pilot holes for No. 8 or smaller screws with an awl. For larger sizes, drill holes with a power or hand drill.

When do you need a pilot hole?

If there is a danger of cracking the wood, you should always drill a pilot hole, no matter how small the screw. For instance, if the wood is brittle or if you are driving a screw near the end of a board, almost any screw can split the wood. But if you are screwing into a sound board at a spot 2 inches or more from its end, you can probably drive a No. 6 or thinner screw without a pilot hole. If you are screwing into plywood or framing lumber, you should be able to drive No. 8 screws without pilot holes. When you drive brass or aluminum screws for latches and decorative hardware, always drill a pilot hole. To further ensure against breaking soft-metal screws, drive a steel screw of the same size into the hole first.

Drilling pilot holes

To see if a drill bit is the correct size to make your pilot hole, grip both bit and screw together with your fingers. The bit should be slightly smaller than the diameter of the screw threads. The diameter of a pilot hole varies depending on the wood. You can drill a smaller hole in softwood than you would in hardwood. Drill a test hole and make sure the screw will hold tight before you drill holes in the finished material.

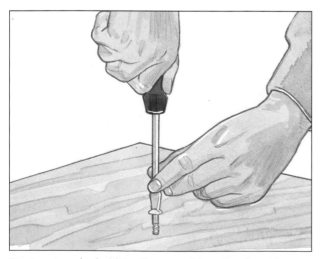

Start a screw by holding the screwdriver handle and blade. Don't hold the screw.

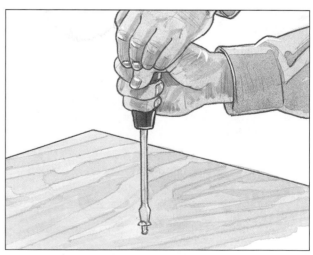

Put more drive on the screwdriver by turning it with one hand and applying top pressure with the other.

When a screw won't turn

If a screw is very hard to drive, make sure the tip of the blade fully fills the screw slot. Try using a longer screwdriver or one with a larger-diameter handle. Another trick to try is to rub wax on the threads of the screw as a lubricant.

Power-driving screws

Even a few screws can take a long time to drive by hand, so consider using a variable-speed drill with a screwdriver bit. If the drill is reversible, so much the better because you can also use it to remove screws.

When driving slotted screws, make sure the bit does not wander partway out of the slot, or you could damage the surface into which you are screwing. Don't drive screws too quickly, or the bit may slip out of the slot. Maintain firm, even pressure as you work.

A popular screwdriver accessory for a drill/driver accepts interchangeable bits in a magnetic holder. The magnetized bit holds steel screws, making it easy to drive them in hard-to-reach places. A sliding sleeve on the tool also helps hold the screw in place for easier starting. To change bits for different kinds of screws, just pull one out and slip another into the holder.

Have a collection of screwdriver tips ready, particularly #1 and #2 phillips bits and some slotted bits as well. Consider buying square-head screws and bits. These bits fit into and grab the screw slot better than phillips-head and slotted screws and bits.

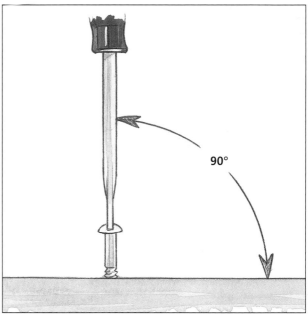

Keep the screwdriver square in the slot. If it's off-center or at an angle, it may slip out and badly strip the slot.

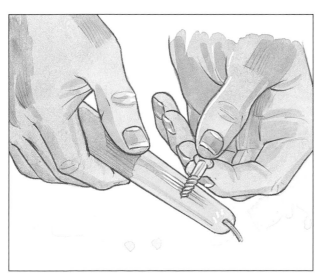

Screws drive easier when threads are lubricated with candle wax. Rotate the screw as you rub it against the candle.

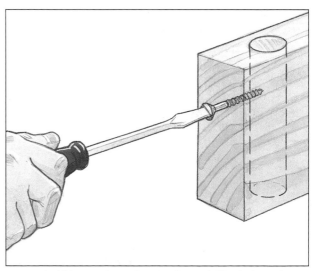

Screws hold better in end grain if you drill a hole and insert a dowel into the board. Use screws long enough to penetrate the dowel.

FASTENING WITH BOLTS

Friction between the fastener and the wood makes nails and screws work. When you tighten a nut on a bolt, however, you're actually clamping adjoining members together, producing the sturdiest of all joints. All types of bolts require a hole to be bored through both pieces being joined.

Be careful: Overtightening bolts can strip threads and damage wood, reducing the holding power of a bolt. Tighten the nut and bolt firmly against the wood, give the nut another half turn, then stop.

Machine bolts

Machine bolts have hexagonal heads and threads running partway or all the way along the shank. When fastening two pieces of wood together, slip a flat washer onto the bolt and slide the bolt through the holes in both pieces of material. Add another flat washer, then a lock washer. The flat washer keeps the nut and the bolt head from digging into the wood. The lock washer prevents the nut from coming loose. Use two wrenches, one to hold the bolt and the other to draw the nut down onto the bolt.

Countersunk bolts

Use a socket wrench to install a machine bolt in a hard-to-get-at place or when the bolt head is countersunk into a hole in the wood.

Carriage bolts

A carriage bolt has a plain, round head. Insert it into the hole and tap the head flush with the surface. Slip a flat washer, a lock washer, and a nut onto the bolt. Tighten the nut. The square or hexagonal shoulder under the bolt head keeps the bolt from spinning as the nut is tightened. No washer is needed under the head. The lock washer should keep the bolt from working loose. As added protection, you can thread another nut onto the bolt, snug it against the first, then jam the two together by turning them in opposite directions.

MACHINE BOLT

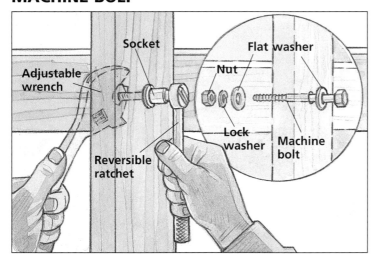

Adjustable wrench · Socket · Nut · Flat washer · Reversible ratchet · Lock washer · Machine bolt

COUNTERSUNK BOLT

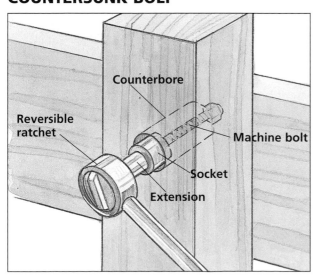

Reversible ratchet · Counterbore · Machine bolt · Socket · Extension

CARRIAGE BOLT

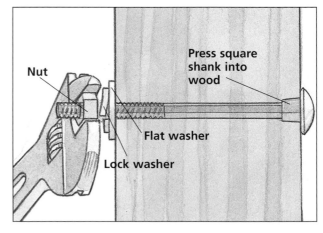

Nut · Press square shank into wood · Flat washer · Lock washer

GLUING AND CLAMPING

A joint will be stronger if you use glue in addition to nails or screws. Glue alone will be enough for joints that will not be subjected to great stress. Use exterior woodworking glue or construction adhesive for outdoor projects. Many adhesives set up quickly, but you still need an assortment of clamps for gluing.

Spring clamps

For light work, these are the easiest clamps to use. Apply glue to both pieces and place them in correct alignment. Squeeze the clamp handles to spread the jaws. When you release the handles, the springs will clamp the work together. You may want to have several sizes of these inexpensive clamps on hand. Thickness capacities range from 1 to 3 inches, and lengths from 4 to 9 inches.

C-clamps

C-clamps are inexpensive and work well when the pieces are not too wide. Use scraps of wood to keep the clamps from marring the boards. C-clamps range in size from 1 to 8 inches with throat depths ranging from 1 to 3½ inches. You can also buy special deep-throat clamps.

Miter clamps

For miter joints, use miter clamps that hold boards at a 90-degree angle. Miter clamps are sometimes called picture-frame clamps. They have smooth jaws that won't mar wood.

Pipe clamps

For large projects, use pipe clamps. Alternate them as shown at *right* to prevent buckling. They're sold without pipe, so you'll need to buy galvanized steel pipe in the lengths you want. The clamp parts fit ½- or ¾-inch pipe.

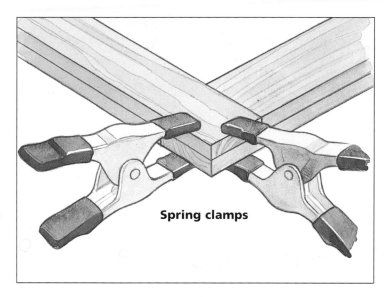

Spring clamps

Strap clamps

A strap, or band, clamp wraps around objects to be joined and is especially handy for holding together irregular parts. It can clamp several joints at once and will not mar the wood.

CLAMPS

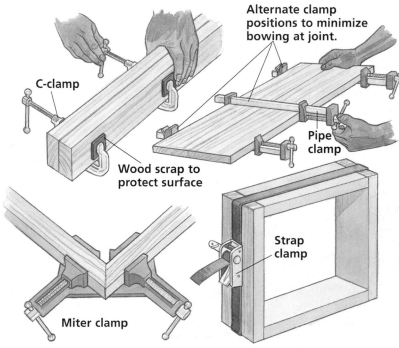

C-clamp

Wood scrap to protect surface

Alternate clamp positions to minimize bowing at joint.

Pipe clamp

Miter clamp

Strap clamp

MAKING LATTICE PANELS

Lacy latticework graces many a trellis, arbor, or pergola, providing peek-through panels that roses and vines can't resist climbing.

1 Begin by building a lightweight 2×2 frame to fit exactly between your posts. Use string to measure the distance between each pair of posts. The horizontal distance between the tops and bottoms of a pair of posts may vary if the posts aren't plumb.

2 Painting is easier before the lattice is assembled, as shown in Step 2, *opposite.* Paint assembled lattice with a roller and touch up edges with a brush.

3 When building lattice panels for exterior projects, use galvanized box nails. Hot-dipped galvanized nails are ideal because their rough surfaces grip the wood better. You'll need a half pound of 3d nails to assemble a 4×8-foot section of lattice.

4 After attaching the lath to the frame, use a straightedge or chalk line to mark across the top and bottom of the lattice panel, flush with the outer edge of the frame. Double-check to make sure no nailheads will be in the path of the saw. The frame serves as a cutting guide.

5 Trim the lattice with a circular saw or a handsaw with a wide blade. If you are using a circular saw, adjust it to cut no deeper than the layers of lath, as shown in the inset illustration for Step 5. With a handsaw, you should be able to just graze the edge of the frame as you trim. Use a fine-tooth blade for easy cutting and a smooth edge.

6 Adding trim around the top and sides gives the lattice panel a more finished appearance. It also holds the lattice onto the frame, increasing rigidity.

KEEP LATTICE FRAMEWORK SQUARE

When you build a framework for a lattice-paneled project, diagonal braces running to stakes, posts, or other stable nailing points will help you plumb the supports. The braces will also keep the frame square until the concrete sets and you have time to firmly attach the panels. Then you can pry off the braces. To provide more rigidity in high-wind areas, run permanent horizontal stringers (2×4s) across the top of the posts and below the panels.

LATTICE PANELS: STEP-BY-STEP

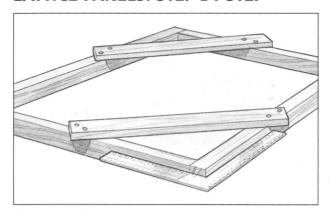

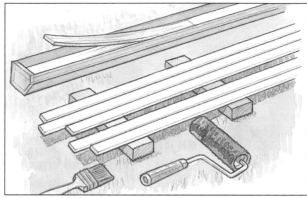

1 To keep the frame straight while you are working, tack scraps of wood diagonally to the back. Turn the frame over to apply the wood strips. Then remove the braces.

2 The quickest way to paint lattice is by dipping the lath in paint before assembly. A length of 4-inch rain gutter capped at both ends makes an ideal dipping tank. Or lay the lath across scraps of wood and paint with a roller.

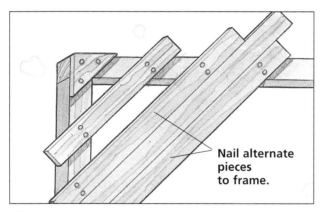

Nail alternate pieces to frame.

3 To assemble the lattice panel, lay the strips of lath on the frame, edge to edge, diagonally. When you have covered a space, nail every other strip. Then remove the pieces that are not nailed. Repeat this process for the second layer of lattice, placing it at a right angle to the first layer.

4 After attaching the lath to the frame, mark the lattice panel for trimming flush with the outside edge of the frame. Use a chalk line or straightedge for accuracy.

Saw blade just clears lath thickness

5 After solidly positioning the panel on sawhorses or another raised base, cut the lattice flush with the frame. You will cut through two layers of lattice.

6 Any molding with a 90-degree corner that will fit flush against the lattice can be used for trim. Strips of lath are often used as trim for lattice panels.

LOCATING AND INSTALLING POSTS

ost of the projects in this book call for posts to be set in straight lines and with square corners. You can do that with a few 1×2s, some mason's twine, and simple arithmetic.

The illustrations on these pages show the essential steps in locating and lining up your posts. Before you start, check with the city or county zoning office to make sure your project will comply with building codes and ordinances regarding setback from your property line. Most locations have a single phone number you can call to have the buried pipes and wires on your property located and marked before you dig. Your local electric utility can probably provide the number. If you can't find the number, call the North American One Call Referral System at 888/258-0808.

LOCATING AND INSTALLING POSTS: STEP-BY-STEP

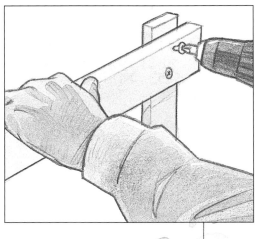

1 Attach a crosspiece to stakes with screws as shown. Use a framing square to help you set the corner's other batterboard at a right angle to the first. When you have installed all your batterboards, wrap a length of mason's twine several times around a crosspiece, pull it tight to the facing batterboard at an adjacent corner, and wrap it there.

2 Measure from one corner of your planned structure to a point 3 feet away on one string and mark the spot on a piece of masking tape folded over the string. Then measure the perpendicular string 4 feet out from the corner and mark that point. Measure between your two marks. If that distance equals 5 feet, the corner is square (90 degrees).

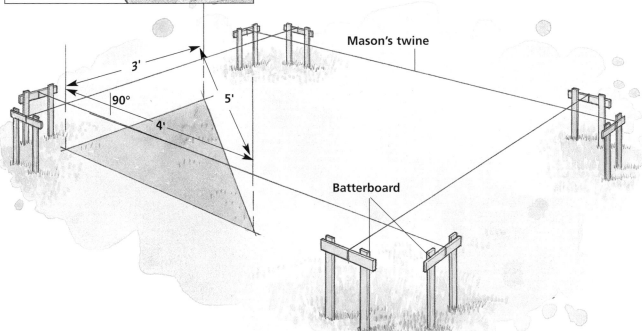

Mason's twine

3'

90°

5'

4'

Batterboard

Get organized

You need little equipment to lay out posts for an outdoor structure. For an easy way to visualize its size and shape, use a tape measure and a garden hose to outline your project's dimensions on the ground. Then gather some 1×2 lumber; cut it into 3-foot lengths for *batterboards*. You also will need a heavy hammer to drive the upright stakes into the ground, a cordless drill/driver, a plumb bob, a spool of mason's twine, and 1½-inch deck screws for quick assembly.

You'll need a posthole digger, shovel, level, hammer, circular saw for trimming posts to length, tamping rod or board, and, if you're mixing your own concrete, a wheelbarrow or mixing box and a concrete hoe.

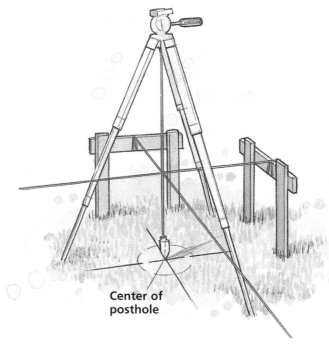

Center of posthole

3 At each corner, transfer the strings' intersections to the ground with mason's line and a plumb bob. A camera or telescope tripod makes a handy holder. Keep the line about ⅛ inch away from the strings so that you don't push them out of position. The plumb bob points to the spot where the center of the post will be.

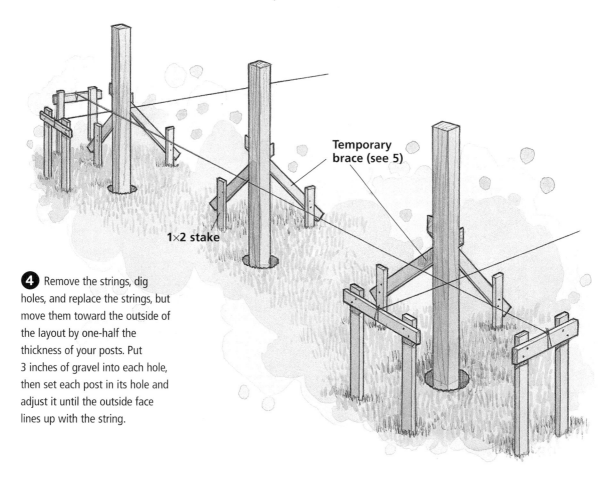

Temporary brace (see 5)

1×2 stake

4 Remove the strings, dig holes, and replace the strings, but move them toward the outside of the layout by one-half the thickness of your posts. Put 3 inches of gravel into each hole, then set each post in its hole and adjust it until the outside face lines up with the string.

SETTING POSTS IN CONCRETE

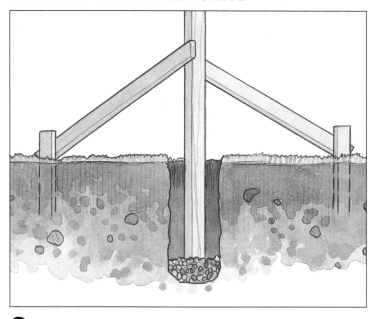

5 The 3-inch layer of gravel in the hole drains water away from the post base to help prevent rot. Set the post in place, plumb it on two sides, and brace it with outriggers in opposite directions. If you've dug the posthole too deep, use a rock as a shim. If a hole is too shallow, dig deeper or saw off the post top.

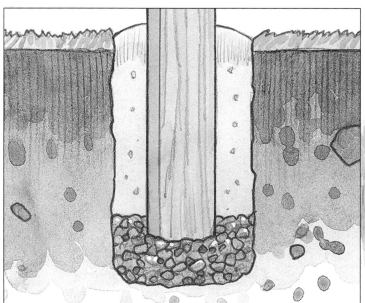

6 Add more gravel around the post. Mix and pour in concrete, tamping as you fill to remove air bubbles from the mix. Mound concrete around the top of the hole as shown. This drains away water that might otherwise pool and cause rot. After the concrete sets, remove the outriggers.

Posts set in the ground and anchored with concrete are the best way to support a gate, large arbor, or pergola. For a lighter structure, especially one you might decide to move later, you can simply set posts in earth, as shown on page 166.

Define each corner with a pair of batterboards. For each batterboard, make a pair of stakes by cutting a point on one end of two 1×2s. Attach a crossbar (see Step 1), and drive the batterboards into the ground. Set them 2 feet away from the planned corner location.
Locate them so that a line connecting the posthole centerlines will be at about the center of the crossbar.

7 For a watertight seal around posts in concrete, apply butyl caulk around the post base after the concrete cures. This assures that even if a post shrinks a bit over time, it will be protected against rot. Use only cedar or redwood heartwood posts or lumber that has been pressure treated for ground contact.

However you decide to set your posts, be sure to dig holes for them 6 inches deeper than the frost line in your area to counter the effects of frost heaving. Dig an 8-inch-diameter hole for each 4×4 post, using a power auger, hand auger, or posthole digger (see page 130–131). A 6×6 post requires a 10-inch-diameter hole. For a neater job and added protection against heaving, line the postholes with cardboard form tubes (available at home centers) before you pour in the concrete.

Concrete choices

Because the posts are set one at a time, consider buying premixed bags of concrete. Premixed material has the correct amount of sand and gravel added to the cement; all you do is add water and mix.

Or buy the cement in bags, order sand and gravel, and mix the concrete yourself. Mixing it yourself is less expensive, but the convenience of premixed concrete is usually worth the extra money. In either case, you will need gravel for the bottom of the postholes.

Mixing concrete

For most post-setting projects, use the standard mix of three parts gravel mix, two parts sand, and one part cement. When mixed with water, this mixture contains enough cement to coat each particle of sand and gravel, creating the bond that gives concrete its strength.

If you mix your own concrete, move the mixing container as close to your posts as possible. This will allow you easy access to keep the mixture thick and strong, yet workable.

Mixing concrete is a lot like mixing cake batter. You have to follow the recipe (or adapt it slightly) to obtain the very best results. Just as you can ruin a cake by adding too much liquid,

you can weaken concrete if you add too much water in proportion to the other materials. On the other hand, too little water makes the concrete difficult to pour.

The amount of water needed depends on the sand. You'll need less water with wet sand than with dry sand. Test the wetness by balling some sand in your hand. If water runs out, the sand is too wet. If the ball compacts like moist clay, the sand is too dry. As you mix the concrete, add very small amounts of water at a time. The concrete may crumble at first, but as you add more water, it will begin to flow together like mud. When it becomes one color—medium gray—and has a plasticlike sheen, it's ready.

EMBEDDED BASES

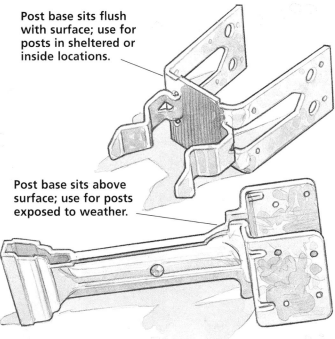

Post base sits flush with surface; use for posts in sheltered or inside locations.

Post base sits above surface; use for posts exposed to weather.

Set embedded bases like the ones shown here into the concrete as you pour your footing. They must be accurately positioned and held in place as the concrete cures. Use a standoff base like the bottom one in the illustration for outdoor posts. For other post bases, see pages 166–167.

Setting posts in concrete for a light-duty structure, such as a trellis or a simple arbor, is often unnecessary. You can save yourself the trouble of mixing concrete by simply digging holes, setting posts into the holes, and filling around them with earth. And with a drive-in post anchor like the one shown *below right*, you don't even have to dig holes.

Setting posts in earth

As with posts set in concrete, dig holes deep enough to go 6 inches below the frost line, then add several inches of gravel to the bottoms of the holes. Posts in shallower holes or without the gravel can easily be knocked out of plumb by frost heave.

Set a post in place, plumb it, and brace it with outriggers, as shown on page 163. Then slowly shovel soil into the hole on all sides of the post, firmly tamping it down as you go. (A length of 2×4 makes a good tamper.) After you've completely filled the hole, mound earth around the post's base. This drains water away from the post base, minimizing chances for rot at that critical point. After several rainfalls, check the mounded earth. If it has settled, rebuild the mound and firmly compact it.

Steely solutions

If you're setting posts atop an existing patio, deck, or porch, steel post bases and anchors may be your only option. Some post bases, shown on page 165, are made to be embedded in wet concrete. Others bolt to existing concrete. Some of these establish a standoff distance of about 1 inch between the bottom of

SETTING POSTS IN EARTH

To set posts in soil, lay a gravel base, then shovel dirt into the hole, tamping it to compact the earth firmly around the post. A string and line level attached to the post top and the top of a post you've already set assures that the tops are even.

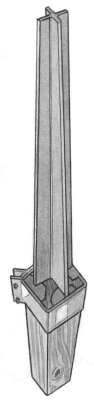

One type of anchor, the GroundTech post installation device, shown above, drives into the ground without digging. You tighten two bolts on the steel fixture to clamp the post into its collar.

SETTING POSTS ON CONCRETE OR WOOD

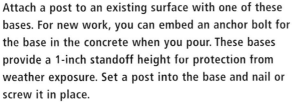

Attach a post to an existing surface with one of these bases. For new work, you can embed an anchor bolt for the base in the concrete when you pour. These bases provide a 1-inch standoff height for protection from weather exposure. Set a post into the base and nail or screw it in place.

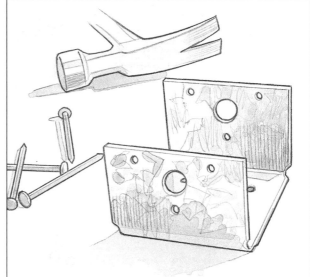

A plain U-shape base doesn't raise the bottom of the post above ground level, so water could collect there. Avoid using this style for outdoor projects unless the post base will be protected from moisture. Nail the base in place, drill a hole through the post, slide a long bolt through the base and post, and secure with a washer and nut.

the post and the concrete, which keeps the foot of the post above ground moisture and puddled water, reducing the risk of rot.

The base attaches to concrete with a ½-inch bolt 5 inches long. To install the bolt, drill a hole for it in the concrete, then cement it into the hole with mortar or an epoxy masonry adhesive. Set the bolt so that the end extends about ¾ inch above the surface.

After the mortar or epoxy cures, secure the base with a nut and washer. Then position the post in the base and nail or screw it in place.

You can also use steel anchors to join posts to another wooden structure, such as a deck or porch. Just nail or screw the base to the surface. A simple U-shape base will work where no moisture protection standoff is necessary.

Anchor answers

When building and anchoring a structure, keep these points in mind:

■ Check building codes for particular requirements or limitations.

■ The post bases shown are recommended for anchoring posts that have a supporting top-structure.

■ Always use the number and size of fasteners specified for the base. Don't substitute drywall screws for nails; use screws of the type and size specified by the base manufacturer.

■ Outdoors or where water may splash onto the foot of the post, install a base that raises the bottom of the post about 1 inch above the surface. This prevents water from puddling around the bottom of the post and wicking into the end grain.

Smoothing Outdoor Projects

Once you've taken the time to cut and assemble your project, don't rush through the final steps–sanding and, if necessary, planing. If you use a belt sander with a rough abrasive, you can remove about ⅛ inch of material. To remove more, plane it first, then sand.

Using a plane

The keys to using a plane are balance and rhythm. Plant both feet firmly on the floor so you can take smooth, even cutting strokes with the plane. You should produce thin, unbroken shavings that are all the same thickness. If the shavings are thick and thin or if they crumble and break apart, the plane *iron* (the blade) is probably dull or improperly set, or you're off balance and jabbing the blade into the work.

As a general rule, plane wood just short of the scribed finish line you want to match. Finish the job with an abrasive material over a sanding block so you can keep it square to the work.

Using abrasives

Sandpaper–also called coated abrasive–prepares wood for its final finish. Don't expect

PLANING

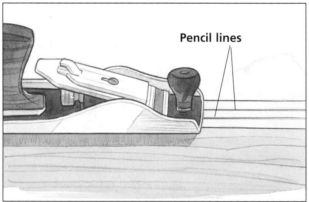

Draw pencil lines on the edge of the piece to be planed. Use them to help locate high spots as you work. Draw another line on the side of the board to serve as the finish line you want to reach.

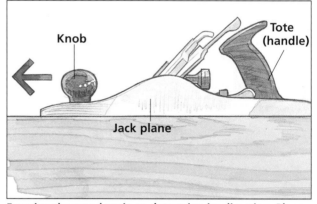

Examine the wood grain to determine its direction. Plane with the grain to minimize snagging and tear-out. Plane just short of the finish line and finish the job with sandpaper.

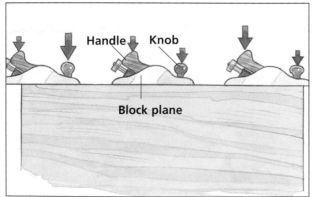

Begin the stroke by applying most of the pressure to the knob. Equalize pressure on the plane fore and aft in the center of the stroke. Complete the stroke with more pressure on the handle.

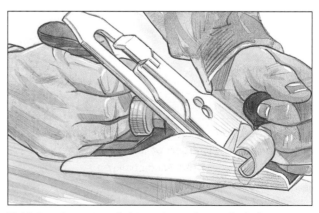

Hold the plane at a slight angle to the work. A sharp plane, properly used, will shave off continuous ribbons of wood. Plane end grain from the sides to the middle to avoid splintering wood at the edge.

stain, varnish, or paint to cover up a rough surface for you. They will only follow the contours of the wood and often will accentuate, rather than hide, imperfections.

Take the time and trouble to sand three times, using progressively finer sandpaper. The wood surface may feel smooth after your first and second sandings, but it will get smoother as you move on to finer-grit sandpapers. A common progression is to start with 80-grit paper, followed by 120-grit and 180-grit. You can sand to 220-grit, but that is not usually necessary for outdoor projects. Clean dust from the wood between sandings.

If you can't sand out a stain or discoloration, apply a small amount of laundry bleach to the stain. Repeat until you get the right color.

Power sanding

Portable electric sanders supply the continuous muscle power that you need for sanding projects. Just flip the starter switch, press down lightly, and steer. In fact, this equipment does such an efficient job of quickly removing material and smoothing, your biggest problem may be controlling the machine.

■ **Be careful:** When sanding, particularly with power tools, wear a face mask. To avoid getting dust in the house, close doors and windows near the work site.

SANDING

Except in hard-to-reach areas, never use abrasive sheets alone, always use some sort of sanding block, either readymade or improvised. Sanding with a block is less tiring and produces more uniform results. Sand only in the direction of the wood grain; sanding across the grain or in a circular motion can leave hard-to-remove scratches. If you use the right grade of paper, light strokes are all you'll need.

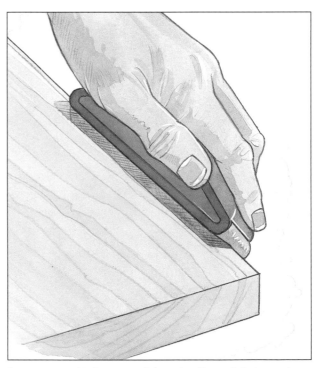

Because wood edges can nick and splinter, it is a good idea to round them off with a light sanding. Hold the sanding block at an angle; use gentle pressure and a rocking motion. A molded rubber sanding block like the one shown is ideal because its base gives only slightly.

FINISHING OUTDOOR PROJECTS

Outdoor projects have to withstand more abuse than their indoor counterparts. Here's how to select a durable finish that's right for your trellis, arbor, or pergola.

Redwood, cedar, or pressure-treated wood left unfinished will soon take on the weathered look, complete with natural checks and slight surface imperfections. The wood will eventually turn gray—a color unappealing to many that signals the first stage in wood deterioration. If you prefer the rich, natural hue of brand new lumber, apply a product that forms a film on the surface of the wood. The film must stand up to harsh outdoor conditions.

Wood left outdoors has two formidable foes: moisture and the ultraviolet (UV) rays in sunlight. Different exterior finishes provide different degrees of protection against them. Here's a survey of your choices:

Clear finishes for natural colors

Spar varnish, polyurethane varnish, water repellents, and penetrating oils shield wood from water while allowing all the color to show through. But clear finishes let UV rays penetrate into the grain. The wood cells react with these rays and begin to deteriorate under the film. The wood darkens, and the finish cracks, blisters, and peels.

Adding a UV filtering agent to the finish retards this reaction but doesn't completely eliminate it. If you use a clear finish, select one that has UV absorbers (the label will tell you). Even with UV protection, you'll have to reapply the finish at least every two years. If you wait until it peels, you'll face a tedious stripping job.

Semitransparent stains

With light pigmentation, semitransparent stains let the wood's natural grain and texture show through. These stains are available in tones that closely match various woods. Brighter stains can either contrast with or complement your house, deck, or patio. Semitransparent stains usually have an oil base and only fair resistance to UV rays, so you'll have to recoat the project every year or two.

Semisolid stains have more pigment than semitransparent stains and offer more UV resistance as well. But they're not completely opaque. You can expect a semisolid stain to last about two years.

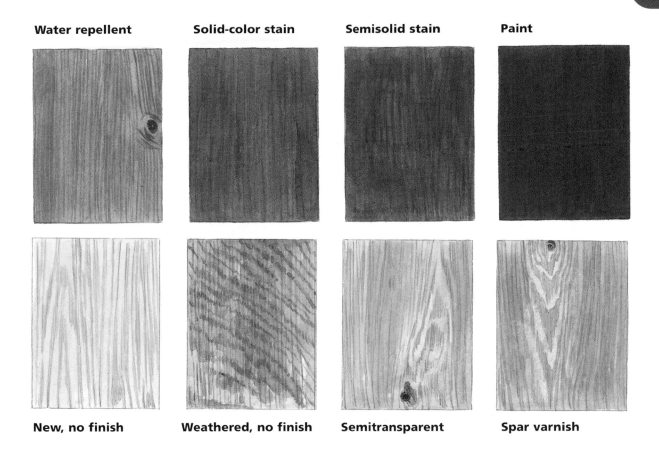

Water repellent	Solid-color stain	Semisolid stain	Paint
New, no finish	Weathered, no finish	Semitransparent	Spar varnish

Opaque stains

Opaque stains, like paint, conceal the wood's natural color, yet they allow the texture to show. They're available in a variety of natural-looking colors and brighter hues and with either an oil or latex base. You also can choose either a flat opaque stain or a low-luster finish that's easier to wash.

Because the pigment in this type of stain is suspended in an oil or latex carrier, it's possible that it won't penetrate all wood surfaces equally. On horizontal surfaces especially, pigment that doesn't completely penetrate may collect, causing blotchy areas that wear off or blister. The California Redwood Association doesn't recommend using stains with a latex base on redwood products. Opaque stains usually need to be recoated every two years.

You need to select a compatible stain color for treated lumber because the chemical used to treat the wood imparts a color of its own that tends to alter the final appearance. You might want to experiment with several different stain colors on treated wood (use scraps left from the project) until you achieve the effect you want. (Some manufacturers offer special 4-ounce samples that you can experiment with before selecting a particular product.)

Paint

Paint is rarely used on the top grades of redwood or cedar because it hides grain, texture, and color. But it can be your solution to hiding the hue of treated wood, and it's the only way to protect metal parts.

FINISHING TOOLS AND FINISHES

If you decide to paint a wooden outdoor project, no matter what wood you've selected, be sure to apply an oil- or alkyd-base primer, then sand slightly before the finish coat for better adhesion. For metal, use a primer or finish coat that contains a rust inhibitor.

Horizontal surfaces will probably sustain much more wear and tear than vertical surfaces. Avoid the need for early renewal by selecting the highest-quality exterior-grade enamel available. You'll need to repaint every two to three years.

And finally, while all of these products retard or prevent deterioration, none of them succeed completely (or for very long) without recoating.

Lighten up with bleach

Stains put color into wood. Bleaches take it out, letting you lighten almost any wood to nearly white. Use the right type of bleach for the job. Two-part bleach (sodium hydroxide and hydrogen peroxide) removes the natural color from wood. Chlorine bleach removes dye from

wood, just as it removes color from laundry. Oxalic acid removes rust and water stains. Whichever type you use, neutralize it afterward, following the manufacturer's instructions, sand lightly, then protect the wood with a clear finish.

Laying it on

After you've decided on a finish for your trellis, arbor, or pergola, you need to figure out how you're going to get it from the can onto the wood. The applicator that's right for this job depends partly on the finish you've chosen, partly on the amount of surface you have to cover, and partly on the look you want. Here are your options:

■ **Brushes:** These trusty tools get the nod for most finishing chores. Purchase brushes with synthetic bristles (nylon, polyester, or nylon/polyester blend) for water-base finishes and latex paints, and natural bristles (animal hair) for oil-base finishes and paints. The pores of natural bristles absorb water readily, making

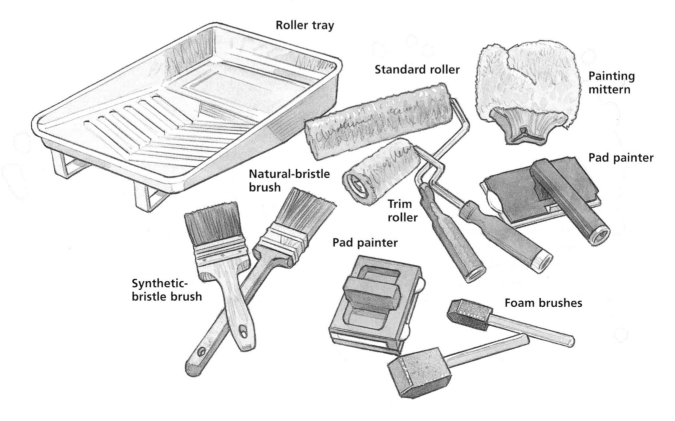

Roller tray

Standard roller

Painting mittern

Pad painter

Natural-bristle brush

Trim roller

Synthetic-bristle brush

Pad painter

Foam brushes

them puffy and hard to control. Oil-base finishes will attack and break down synthetic bristles, so you'll end up with bristles sticking to the surface. Disposable foam brushes work fine with either type of finish and do an especially good job with stains.

■ **Rollers:** Rollers make short work of large, flat surfaces, and you can buy smaller trim rollers for tight spots. Both types have a plastic or wood handle (often threaded to accept an extension pole) and a metal frame that holds the napped cover.

The type of finish (water- or oil-base) determines the type of roller cover to use. Most covers are made from mohair, lamb's wool, acetate, or polyurethane foam and are labeled as to which finish they are appropriate for.

Roller covers vary in nap depths from 1/16 inch to 1½ inches. Use a long-nap roller for rough surfaces, a short-nap one for smooth work. The nap in turn is fastened to a cardboard or plastic sleeve. If you use a water-base finish, buy a roller with a plastic sleeve. For an oil-base finish, get one with a cardboard sleeve.

■ **Pads and Mittens:** Pad painters have a carpetlike material or plastic foam inserted in a plastic, moplike applicator or a paintbrush handle. Though excellent for applying paint to almost any surface, they work especially well on irregular surfaces such as shakes, fencing, screening, and lattice.

A painting mitten makes coating railings, spindles, and similar items easy. Simply put on a thin, disposable plastic glove to keep your hand clean, then put on the thick-nap mitten and dip the mitten into the finish. You can quickly coat a railing or spindle by grasping it and sliding the mitten along its length. And you can poke finish into narrow or cramped places where a brush would spatter.

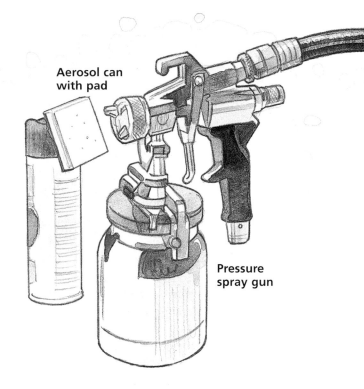

Aerosol can with pad

Pressure spray gun

■ **Sprayers:** For a smooth, rich finish that goes on quickly, consider spraying your project with an aerosol spray can or an air-operated spray gun. Spraying can be messy, of course, but some aerosol sprays shoot finish through a pad like the one on a pad painter.

Pressurized equipment has become neater too, thanks to high-volume, low-pressure (HVLP) equipment, which wastes less finish and reduces overspray. Conventional spray guns blast out air at up to 40 pounds per square inch (psi). HVLP units need only 4 to 10 psi to get the job done, so up to 85 percent of the finish lands on the workpiece instead of the 36 percent with conventional sprayers. (The percentage that doesn't go onto the project goes into the air as overspray and settles on everything else in the vicinity.)

INDEX

METRIC CONVERSIONS

U.S. Units to Metric Equivalents			Metric Units to U.S. Equivalents		
To Convert From	Multiply By	To Get	To Convert From	Multiply By	To Get
Inches	25.4	Millimeters	Millimeters	0.0394	Inches
Inches	2.54	Centimeters	Centimeters	0.3937	Inches
Feet	30.48	Centimeters	Centimeters	0.0328	Feet
Feet	0.3048	Meters	Meters	3.2808	Feet
Yards	0.9144	Meters	Meters	1.0936	Yards
Square inches	6.4516	Square centimeters	Square centimeters	0.1550	Square inches
Square feet	0.0929	Square meters	Square meters	10.764	Square feet
Square yards	0.8361	Square meters	Square meters	1.1960	Square yards

To convert from degrees Fahrenheit (F) to degrees Celsius (C), first subtract 32, then multiply by ⅚.

To convert from degrees Celsius to degrees Fahrenheit, multiply by ⅚, then add 32.

USDA PLANT HARDINESS ZONE MAP

T his map of climate zones helps you select plants for your garden that will survive a typical winter in your region. The United States Department of Agriculture (USDA) developed the map, basing the zones on the lowest recorded temperatures across North America. Zone 1 is the coldest area and Zone 11 is the warmest.

Plants are classified by the coldest temperature and zone they can endure. For example, plants hardy to Zone 6 survive where winter temperatures drop to –10° F. Those hardy to Zone 8 die long before it's that cold. These plants may grow in colder regions but must be replaced each year. Plants rated for a range of hardiness zones can usually survive winter in the coldest region as well as tolerate the summer heat of the warmest one.

To find your hardiness zone, note the approximate location of your community on the map, then match the color band marking that area to the key.

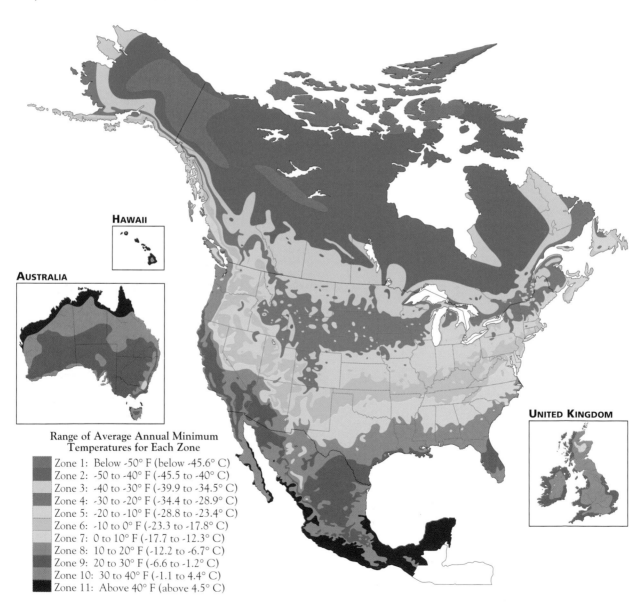

HAWAII

AUSTRALIA

UNITED KINGDOM

Range of Average Annual Minimum Temperatures for Each Zone

Zone 1: Below -50° F (below -45.6° C)
Zone 2: -50 to -40° F (-45.5 to -40° C)
Zone 3: -40 to -30° F (-39.9 to -34.5° C)
Zone 4: -30 to -20° F (-34.4 to -28.9° C)
Zone 5: -20 to -10° F (-28.8 to -23.4° C)
Zone 6: -10 to 0° F (-23.3 to -17.8° C)
Zone 7: 0 to 10° F (-17.7 to -12.3° C)
Zone 8: 10 to 20° F (-12.2 to -6.7° C)
Zone 9: 20 to 30° F (-6.6 to -1.2° C)
Zone 10: 30 to 40° F (-1.1 to 4.4° C)
Zone 11: Above 40° F (above 4.5° C)